'George Lings is as per... what the ancient idea c... today. Whether you are ...ie or your church community, this ... ...t.h reading. There is a wealth of practical experience in this book which can bring change and transformation for you and your church.'
Revd Dave Male, director of evangelism and discipleship for the Church of England

'In this extremely helpful book, George Lings explores how sacred spaces and intentional forms of Christian community can be re-harmonised with the needs of the contemporary world. His use of the seven spaces is a useful way to explore the significance, possibilities and opportunities under the guidance of the Holy Spirit to reimagine how the church can be contextualised and buildings brought back to life.'
Ian Mobsby, assistant dean for fresh expressions in the Diocese of Southwark, guardian of the New Monastic Society of the Holy Trinity and interim pioneer rector at Christ Church Southwark

'This book is knowledgeable, quirky and inspirational. The seven sacred spaces are drawn from their monastic roots to provide a framework for discipleship, Christian community and wider human well-being. As someone who has long inhabited the seven sacred spaces in his own discipleship, George Lings enthuses about their potential, illustrating it from the experience of a variety of contemporary expressions of church.'
Sally Gaze, archdeacon for rural mission and leader of the Lightwave Community, Diocese of St Edmundsbury and Ipswich

'In weaving together ancient monastic wisdom, fresh insights from contemporary developments and the author's rich experiences of the adventure of faith, *Seven Sacred Spaces* provides a valuable, timely and practical resource for all on the Jesus Way.'
Steve Aisthorpe, author of *The Invisible Church* and mission development worker for the Church of Scotland

'George Lings is a radical, one who believes that we should explore the deep roots of faith if we are to live well. *Seven Sacred Spaces* distils the wisdom of decades of looking, listening and reflecting. Read it if you want to be a deep-rooted Christian today. I recommend it very, very highly.'
Rt Revd Paul Bayes, Bishop of Liverpool

'Here we are presented with the challenging proposal that the rhythm of monastic life with its seven sacred spaces does not need to be confined to the monastery. Rather it can shape and enrich the lives of men and women of all ages and in all states of life.'
Sister Frances Dominica OBE, DL, founder of Helen House

'In this book, George Lings is like a master chef. Not one of those fancy ones who make things that are only possible in rarefied conditions with unlimited budgets. Rather, like the best specialist, the dish he creates is genius in the simplicity of its ingredients and in the profundity of how they have been put together – you can taste the layers and the richness of it. Drawing on scripture, tradition, attention to conditions and tastes, George adds together these seven ingredients of sacred space and reduces them down with time, wisdom and care into a way of living that makes possible what many of us truly long for – an authentic Jesus-shaped life. I love the book – it's gold.'
Chris Russell, vicar of St Laurence, Reading, and the Archbishop of Canterbury's adviser on evangelism and witness

'In his typical thorough, imaginative and fair way, George Lings explores some essential disciplines from the ancient life and witness of the monastery, and he demonstrates how a grasp of these can radically affect how we live and witness for Christ in today's culture. Anyone reading this will be inspired and challenged by George's fascinating study of each of these sacred spaces.'
Canon Michael Mitton, writer, speaker, spiritual director and canon emeritus at Derby Cathedral

'This book drew me into a world of monastic spaces and monastic practices. Exploring these seven spaces, with current and historic examples, helped me to reflect on the value of these distinctive modes and ways of being church. I highly recommend *Seven Sacred Spaces* to those who are interested in finding out more about monasticism and those imagining how church can develop alongside and beyond the Sunday service. It has certainly helped me to imagine how these spaces and practices could enhance discipleship, community and mission within my own context of a suburban parish church.'
Revd Dr Beth Keith, associate vicar of All Saints Ecclesall Sheffield

'Through personal reflections and informed observations, George Lings gives some timely insights at a moment of global change. As we live our lives in different patterns – isolated, dispersed and online – his reimaging of life through the seven sacred spaces has application in a variety of ways. Noticing that society already echoes these spaces in its architecture, this book outlines how we can embrace them for personal and corporate spiritual renewal. It also highlights a powerful paradigm shift for our approach to mission, inviting us to consider the value of "being" as much as "doing". This is a helpful accompaniment for pioneers as they live out these key questions and seek to reimagine church in new ways.'
Revd Ed Olsworth-Peter, national adviser for pioneer development for the Church of England

'As we discern together fruitful ways forward in the wake of the Covid-19 pandemic, the church urgently needs fresh reflection on the different ways in which we are the body of Christ. George Lings offers this in abundance in *Seven Sacred Spaces*, distilling new wisdom for today from scripture and tradition and many decades of his research and reflection. Every local church community will find here rich inspiration and strong practical support.'
Rt Revd Dr Steven Croft, Bishop of Oxford

The Bible Reading Fellowship
15 The Chambers, Vineyard
Abingdon OX14 3FE
brf.org.uk

The Bible Reading Fellowship (BRF) is a Registered Charity (233280)

ISBN 978 0 85746 934 2
First published 2020
10 9 8 7 6 5 4 3 2 1 0
All rights reserved

Acknowledgements
Unless otherwise stated, scripture quotations are taken from The Holy Bible, New
International Version (Anglicised edition) copyright © 1979, 1984, 2011 by Biblica.
Used by permission of Hodder & Stoughton Publishers, a Hachette UK company.
All rights reserved. 'NIV' is a registered trademark of Biblica. UK trademark
number 1448790.

Scripture quotations marked KJV are taken from the Authorised Version of the
Bible (The King James Bible), the rights in which are vested in the Crown, are
reproduced by permission of the Crown's Patentee, Cambridge University Press.

Scripture quotations marked ESV are taken from the Holy Bible, English Standard
Version, published by HarperCollins Publishers, © 2001 Crossway Bibles, a
division of Good News Publishers. Used by permission. All rights reserved.

Every effort has been made to trace and contact copyright owners for material
used in this resource. We apologise for any inadvertent omissions or errors, and
would ask those concerned to contact us so that full acknowledgement can be
made in the future.

A catalogue record for this book is available from the British Library

Printed and bound by CPI Group (UK) Ltd, Croydon CR0 4YY

George Lings

Seven Sacred Spaces

Portals to deeper
community life in Christ

Contents

Acknowledgements

I am writing this as the full seriousness of the coronavirus pandemic has become clear. Like the psalmist, we too now 'walk through the valley of the shadow of death' (Psalm 23:4). Each person's future has become profoundly uncertain. In addition, locked down in our own homes, we all face the sharp question, 'What will this new isolated life be like?'

My wife Helen and I have taken the insights and balance of living out the seven sacred spaces and have found life and order as they have shaped our day. For us it looks like this:

After breakfast we begin separately with private prayer (Cell). Then for me comes a morning of reading and writing (Scriptorium), followed at noon by shared midday prayer (Chapel), then deliberate quiet. 1.00 pm lunch (Refectory) is followed by varied pieces of work (Garden): household chores, personal email, cleaning the car or bike, cooperating with spring in the garden, developing my model railway and staying fit using our static bike. Evening prayer occurs at 5.30 pm (Chapel again) and supper at 7.00 pm. For the prayer times, rather than nag each other we ring a bell. Come the evening, I have no idea which space corresponds to watching TV – I guess it depends on what sort of programme it is. The day closes with Compline (Chapel again). Living 24 hours a day with one's partner leads to frequent, sometimes demanding, meetings with one another (Cloister). Across the day comes decision-making about what to do or not to do (Chapter).

So in these extraordinary times, the ancient patterns and purposes of monastic life, expressed in the seven sacred spaces, have brought to us a welcome shape and renewed purpose to living.

But none of this would have been written without my colleague and friend Sue Hope, who first pointed out these patterns to me in 2009. I thank her and Church Army, who then gave me a sabbatical that year to study this, and who funded the publishing of my findings.

I thought that was the end of the story, but people round the country started to tell me they were using this insight and it was a portal into a richer communal Christian life. Moreover, Helen has lovingly nagged (no, I should write persistently encouraged) me to turn the 2009 booklet into a book to serve a wider readership. Well done, dear, you were right – again.

I also gladly thank Olivia Warburton at BRF, who rescued what looked like a publishing idea that had died. She steered me through the writing process, with warm encouragement and judicious cutting.

Lastly my thanks to many people who gave me their stories which make up one chapter. This demonstrates that this is no mere theory from an ivory tower. It has been road-tested in the past and now in the present. It is indeed a portal and has been found to be life-giving. I trust that when, please God, the Covid-19 crisis is over, the places, patterns and portal I describe will help in the reordering of our lives in what may be a new era.

Foreword

This excellent book reads like a traveller's guide – an invitation and companion to an adventure and a way of life that is both inspiring and practical, written by someone who has journeyed far and wide in his explorations, a pilgrim who lives what he writes about.

George Lings' exploratory inquisitiveness and astute observational eye for detail have contributed to a thorough analysis of the seven sacred spaces. Insightful and informative, this book goes beyond ideas and expressions to reveal the values and principles that provide the foundations to a deep yet accessible resource. Mapping out the spaces, their ethos and the importance of environment, location and shapes, it helps the reader to evaluate and reimagine how faith can be integrated into every area of life, personally and communally.

Drawing from the wider riches of monasticism, and his specific experience within the Northumbria Community, George calls the seven spaces 'portals', through which the reader enters and discovers places and spaces to a way of living that nurtures the believer and that also opens up ways for all who are exploring what it means to live life more fully.

This book invites the reader to an adventure through the portal, to explore and discover. Thankfully it's not a book offering another programme, strategy, thing to achieve or box to tick on a list of must-dos. Neither does it provide easy answers or simple how-tos. Rather it awakens curiosity, triggers creativity and encourages some imaginative thinking. If churches, leaders and those training for ministry could be encouraged to use this book as a template to reflect on their life and ministry, the seven spaces could significantly contribute to the much-needed reimagining and reformation of what discipleship and church might become in the years ahead. Practical and down-to-earth habits and patterns are shared and illustrated throughout the book, making the disciplines of the seven spaces accessible.

It is a read that can be challenging and, if taken seriously, will impact our lives both personally and in how we relate to others within our family, friendship, church and wider relationship circles. It is quite a subversive book; it provokes and challenges so many of the ways that have been assumed or inherited that, when examined, do little to help the flourishing of life and relationships with God, self or our neighbour. The book's countercultural nonconformity is a breath of fresh air to stale, moribund spaces that have confined and suppressed life and growth.

In drawing on the good, life-giving values and expressions of monasticism, George offers a spirituality that makes sense of life, making the idea of following Christ compelling. This is a great book: an invaluable travelling companion to a way of life.

Roy Searle is one of the founders of the Northumbria Community and a community elder. A former president of the Baptist Union of Great Britain, he is currently one of the denomination's pioneer ambassadors, a free-church tutor at Cranmer Hall, St John's College, Durham, an associate tutor at Spurgeon's College, London, and a member of the Renovaré board.

✤ 1 ✤

Oh, I see – my own story

I have lived with the approach that I call 'seven sacred spaces' for over a decade. Chapter 2 gives an overview of what I mean by these words and what the seven spaces are, but in coming to write the book I have been fascinated to realise how much of my life has been a preparation for this way of seeing both the church and the Christian life. This chapter tells that story. Readers may well find echoes of their own discoveries and dead ends.

Looking back

Hindsight can be unkind. Looking back, it is quite easy to see what we could have done better. We can wish, on second thoughts, that we hadn't said some unloving words. With the benefit of hindsight, it is puzzling that we did not understand something earlier.

Yet looking back can also be helpful. It can disclose longer patterns and rhythms to our lives that we missed at the time. As soon as we perceive the links, a sense of meaning and purpose grows. More was going on than what seemed at the time to be an unconnected flow of events.

In retrospect, I realise that the seven sacred spaces approach has been creeping up on me for years. It makes sense of a number of chapters in my life which were satisfying and wholesome Christian experiences. It connects to a lifelong aching desire within my spiritual journey, the suspicion that 'there must be more than this'.

For any readers who have given up on church, for those who still attend a congregation but feel they are stuck, for those who sense they trudge a plateau of spiritual mediocrity, that wondering – 'there must be more than this' – will resonate, even if finding any way forward at the moment is elusive.

So how did this richer way of looking at church sneak up on me? 'Church' is a negative word for many people today, for plenty of good reasons. Let me clarify right at the start that when I say 'church', I am not thinking of an institution, a building or an organisation. I think it is most helpful to see church as an interpersonal, Jesus-centred community. If you want to read more about that way of thinking and the difference it makes, you could read chapter 2 of my previous book *Reproducing Churches*.[1] For me, there need be no gap between belonging to Jesus' church and having a shared Christian life worth living. I admit immediately that for many people there is a chasm between these two. My discovery has been to see that the seven sacred spaces approach is one way in which that disturbing gap can close.

Early days at home

I grew up in the London suburb of Barnes, which is like a village. Anyone who watches the annual Oxford and Cambridge boat race will have seen part of it. My brothers and I would watch the early stages on TV, then run down our road and see the crews go by, only to dash back and catch the finish on the telly.

My father, Jim, had been a communist as a student in 1930s Oxford, before fighting in the war and later settling down to become a patent agent. My mum, Hilde, had been a lapsed Catholic German, who came to Britain shortly before the war and settled in Oxford for ten years as an au pair and nanny. They met as friends in that Oxford house. Before going out to fight in India, Jim's CO said to him, 'Lings, get a photo of your wife and children, or your servants won't respect you.' Being single, this was somewhat tricky. So he set up Hilde and the three children she looked after and had the photo taken. I have it still. Perhaps looking at it for five years grew on him. He returned after the war, popped the question in 1948, and they had children. I am the first of three boys. With two such diverse backgrounds, I jest that it was natural that my parents became Anglicans!

My earliest Christian experiences were of weekly attendance in nearby All Saints' Putney, where my father was the treasurer. The tradition was moderately Anglo-Catholic, with a gospel procession and eucharistic vestments but not incense. We prayed from booklets of the 1928 Communion service, in part sung to the music of John Merbecke (1510–85). In those days, children did not even go up to the rails to be blessed, let alone receive. Yet even then, I sensed, as a non-receiver, that there was a transcendence to be respected and a 'more' to enter into, for which people willingly queued up and from which they seemed to return tranquil and helped.

Another inkling of 'more' is my memory, from when I was 6 or 7, of reading an illustrated children's book with my father, based on the Lord's Prayer. The picture that was set alongside its closing words, 'forever and ever', was of a winding path heading off and upwards into the distance. Somehow this planted the beguiling concept and endless attraction of eternity into my child's mind. Even now, at 70, I can honestly say it is pleasing to be nearer to entering that reality which began to beckon me when I was 7. Looking back, it was my first intimation that significant growing in faith could occur outside the church building and its Sunday service.

A surprise gift

The Anglo-Catholic strand to my understanding was laid down first and has gifts that I retain, but it was rudely interrupted when my father drowned on a family holiday in France when I was 7. He and the patent agent firm he worked for had made wise provision against unforeseen disaster, and our ongoing life was secure, if somewhat impoverished. His godmother, Sybil, knowing our straitened circumstances, had connections with the Christian Union of the armed services, the Officers Christian Union (OCU). They ran family summer holidays at boarding schools, to which we were invited, and from 1958 to 1970 these were a highlight of my growing years.

The contrasts were considerable and widened my perception of Christianity and shared Christian life. The leaders were laity, not priests. As officers they were natural leaders and easy to look up to, whereas the ordained priests I knew were pleasant but ethereal. For the first time I had peer-group Christian friends, not just acquaintances to whom you might nod across defended pews on a Sunday. We played games and had fun. I suppose it was muscular Christianity, which is sometimes mocked, but I found it invigorating. There were outings to places of interest; we went exploring, not just to church. These lay leaders gave practical teaching about living as a Christian. They spoke in everyday language. It was possible to discuss and ask questions. The 'quiet time' of personal Bible reading and prayer was commended and practised. This was quite a different way to listen to God compared to hearing an epistle and a gospel in a service. For years, one officer thoughtfully sent me Scripture Union Bible reading notes. The lusty singing came from Children's Special Service Mission choruses. This collection, new to me, was a marked contrast to the Anglican hymn book. They embodied devotion, engagement and first-hand experience of God, whereas many Anglican hymns seemed grand but detached, descriptive but distant.

Looking back now, I know it was a broad evangelicalism, though labels were not used. Their language was simply living Christianity. It was my first taste of what a whole-life Christian community might look like. It wasn't just Christianity as public worship. There was passing on knowledge and experience, and there was time for private prayer, eating together, working at tasks, taking action and relaxing.

As I got older, I qualified for OCU's Easter camp for teenagers. It built upon the same values but intensified the issue of discipleship and raised the question of commitment. On 14 April 1965, I was cornered by an older girl who, to borrow the vocabulary of P.G. Wodehouse, had 'stepped high, wide and plentiful'[2] before 'seeing the light'. She rightly accused me of enjoying all the benefits of camp without the surrender of my own life to Christ. If she should chance to read this – thank you, Jeannie; I still have the *Daily Light* book of daily Bible readings you gave me. As a lifelong believer in God, I don't know if it was a conversion, but it certainly was a commitment. It shifted my experience from intellectual to intimate, from knowing about God to knowing him and being known by him, from guilt to forgiveness and from Christian drabness to consummate joy.

There was a downside which I, and others there, experienced. It was as though we went through an annual Mount of Transfiguration followed by the Slough of Despond[3] a few months later. The loss was so real that a group of us even started our own Christmas reunion to put in an oasis in the long march between summer and the following Easter.

Two changes helped reproduce some of these gains. I left my parents' church, because I was the only teenager there, and went to the neighbouring parish, St Margaret Putney, which included a group of school friends. We went to its evening service, followed by its youth group. From there I was invited to a Sunday afternoon Bible class, then called Crusaders, now renamed Urban Saints. Taken together these two factors added back several features: the peer group element, the building of friendships, receiving teaching appropriate to our age and stage, and importantly taking responsibility for giving some of it. There was even a weekend annual Crusader camp to look forward to.

In 1969 the call to ordination mysteriously arrived, and in 1970 I went, as a very youthful and ignorant 21-year-old, to St John's College, which had newly arrived in Nottingham from London, in buildings not yet quite finished. In that first year, we literally walked on planks across muddy open ground and climbed through a window to get to lectures.

A conscious awakening

The next four years were one of the most consciously constructive periods of my life. My assessment of its genius pays tribute to several aspects. The very talented and diverse staff of St John's College knew the world was changing and did not seek to train us for ordained Anglican ministry as it then was. Rather they trained us to think, going beneath forms to values and principles. They encouraged us to be formed through the experience of community and of mission, not just worship. We also learnt to listen acutely and to discover our true selves.

Those years not only formed my theological instincts, but also led me to be more open to the future, held in conversation with the living Christian tradition. They gave me lifelong friends and a wife, and they planted a desire for a quality of shared and hospitable life that was not only nourishing for the insiders but also attractive and compelling to those looking on from outside. We were a community on an adventure.

Our life together included many elements. Daily morning worship unusually meant meeting in small tutor groups, as well as gathering weekly together in chapel, of which the highlight was the Thursday evening Communion followed by supper. The study element covered expected theological and biblical themes and topics, but in addition we studied philosophy, psychology and education. Our placements could be related to any of these further areas.

The site itself was of diverse spaces. A single-students' block contained 60 individual rooms and a common room for each corridor of twelve people. We experienced being alone and being together.

Across a green courtyard were the married-students' block and the row of staff houses. Along a covered way, shared spaces included a library, a book shop, staff studies and the admin office in one building. The chapel, lecture rooms, refectory, TV room and games room were in another building further along the covered way. I didn't see it at the time, but that palette bearing varied spaces painted a full-colour picture of purposeful communal life. We came out from those years quietly determined to continue those values of diverse communal life ourselves and wondering how these rich gains could be translated to, or awakened in, parish life.

Oxford and Essex

I then took a sideways move after ordination training. My wife Helen and I went to the Oxford Department of Education to study for its certificate. I wanted to study more *how* to communicate, building on *what* I now knew I wanted to communicate. From there I went to a curacy, at St Peter's Harold Wood in Essex. The church was innovative in that its weekly Sunday service was a family service, with both a full illustrated children's talk and an adult sermon. It had an attractional evangelistic life, seeing people come to faith, and a strong sense of family. Curiously, the home Bible groups were deliberately broken up each year, reformed by the ordained staff. Touchy-feely stuff was suspect, and things charismatic were a no-no. Its value of unity trumped any diversity. It was a warm but tight family. It did little towards disclosing seven diverse spaces. After three years it was time to move on.

Seven good years in Reigate

St Mary's Reigate is a large church building and congregation in a Surrey town full of professionals and many London commuters. If labels help, it would be open evangelical and open to the charismatic. But it also had a fiercely defended 1662 Book of Common Prayer

8.00 am Communion service. As a curate once more, I was the youngest member of a talented staff team.

The medieval church was extensively restored in the 19th century. Its space is bicameral (two-roomed) – the nave and the elevated chancel are visually separated by a reputedly medieval wooden screen. In those days the clergy and robed choir peered out through the screen to the populous beyond and below. It was as though the Reformation had never happened. God was still remote, lurking near the sharp end. The space did not model there being one people of God.

The reordering I lived through saw the focal point brought out in front of this screen on a stone apron, the lighting transformed and a simple kitchen and loo facilities installed at the back. We now met and worshipped together in the one nave. It also created a smaller, more intimate worship space in a cleared open chancel with flexible seating. Unworkable complexity had now become diverse flexibility. I learnt that spaces, their location and shapes, all matter.

I was also intrigued by a consistent feature within its 'parish weekends', during which a proportion of the congregation spent the time together at a conference centre. What intrigued me was the quality of the closing service, which combined a touch of transcendence and an aroma of togetherness, never matched on a normal Sunday. Was it because that event was the culmination of having already been together, of having travelled through some corporate spiritual journey, rather than so often on a Sunday trying to start the congregational engine from cold? It raised a beckoning question, rather than giving me an answer.

I was given the youth work, called Spearhead. Knowing my limitations, I recruited a lay couple as fellow youth leaders. Tim and Gay were natural gatherers, carers and evangelists and had a nearby house large enough to accommodate the 50-plus young people who would pile in on a Sunday night. Community flourished in the right sort of space. It took off. Half a dozen of those teenagers are now ordained leaders serving around the country. Both the church redevelopment and the house-based youth work were powerful lessons of how shared church life and the buildings we use to house it intersect. It is no accident that the word 'house' is both a noun and a verb. The right sort of buildings house better belonging.

We also began to learn that big churches only really work as communities if there are effective small groups. Then people don't just join; they make friends. Groups are also spaces in which good public preaching on a Sunday is complemented by the pursuit of discipleship. They become the primary places of belonging and of spiritual growth. This encouraged us to think of our small groups as like tiny churches, practising group worship, teaching, fellowship, mission and ministry. That vision was clear, but its performance across the groups was mixed. Some groups did go deeper, while others remained in Bible-study-only mode. Perhaps it was related to the age groups involved. My generation onwards value emotional intelligence and the appropriate sharing of personal lives. Acquiring more Bible knowledge or dissecting sermons, but remaining personally distant, holds little attraction for us. It was all an education in diverse spaces.

A good Deal

I then became the vicar of St George's Deal in 1985, where we stayed for twelve years. I still gratefully recall how open to reasoned, consensual change the congregation was.

Spaces and location once more played their part. The rare Queen Anne building, with its three-sided gallery, was a natural amphitheatre and preaching box, just off the high street. It fostered openness, communication, celebration and community. Already a 1970 extension had a kitchen, loos, an office and meeting rooms. It was a multi-spaced complex. It expressed who we were growing to be. That was taken further by a 1991 reordering, with warmer adjustable lighting, the opening and carpeting of the chancel, removal of the choir pews and controversially installing a hot-fill baptistery[4] beneath the chancel floor. The area was beautified and made yet more flexible. For example, sacred dance could expansively portray our worship, no longer rather cramped by a tight space.

By 1989 we were full on a Sunday morning and plateaued. A remarkable set of events, way beyond my control, brought Alan and Chris Dodds to us, with a view to starting a church plant. They were good friends with a Church Army background. In 1994 a team of over 30 people was sent out to begin another church based on networks of friendships rather than on geographical area and deliberately for those who did not attend church, rather than existing attenders elsewhere. With the ready agreement of the neighbouring parish, it met in their secular Linwood youth centre.

Here once more, spaces and shapes played a crucial role. The room was set out cafe style, way before that was a known type of fresh expression of church. Tables and chairs provided safe places for people to sit. Snacks, crisps and games already on the tables gave normal activities to children and families, rather than children enduring a tense uncertain wait before a service began.

They were serious about hospitality. From the first, this instinct was expressed by serving drinks as people arrived. This is what happens at secular venues or when people come to our homes. Not for nothing was the church plant called The Carpenters Arms – Jesus does pub, you might say. What a contrast to most churches, where a drink is only offered – often not a great one – at the end. Nor were newcomers given books they might not know their way around; here all you needed came up on a screen. Food, fun, friendliness and a focus on God were combined. In the language of the seven sacred spaces, Refectory and Chapel had been combined, though then I didn't know those terms.

What was important was seeing that a brand-new start opened up very different ways of working. By 1999 they regularly saw 90 adults and 40 children. They too then hit a plateau as growing numbers began to limit the intimacy of the cafe atmosphere. Spaces – what they enable and what happens when we try to overfill them – all matter. So a further plant to neighbouring Sandwich began in 1999, and is connected to St George's Deal even today.

The story in the years after both Alan and I left the area is sad. Yet honesty requires a few headlines. Further leadership did not work out as intended. Subsequent lay leaders became overstretched. Tensions with the diocese led to the church eventually going independent. I learnt the hard way that the right use of spaces does make a vital difference, but it is not a magic bullet. Resources for them, and attitudes of those within them, matter more.

I begin to see more clearly

Significant changes can have unlikely beginnings. In 1996 I wasn't looking to move; further developments at St George's were under way. I just happened to see a *Church Times* advert for a leader for the new Church Army research team, investigating evangelism and church planting. I had no intention to apply, yet I was pleased that someone else would fulfil this role and told my wife so. She told me that I should apply, and then she had to scrape me off the kitchen floor. I was appointed in 1997. I began visiting all kinds of adventurous examples of missional church planting that burst the boundaries of conventional thinking. Two years later a friend persuaded me to write up their stories and capture this learning. The result was the 'Encounters on the Edge' quarterly booklet series that ran from 1999 to 2012.[5]

From 1997 to 2012, I and the slowly growing research team occupied a few offices within the then-residential Church Army training college. We needed to carve out our own space, as we were a distinct team, not an adjunct of the college. We also wanted to make a space that enhanced and expressed our values. We were more than a team; we were a diverse but united community. We turned the largest room into a multi-purpose space. Memorably it housed an L-shaped red sofa, bought initially to the displeasure of our bosses. It became an inviting seat for guests, the cockpit for team discussions, the anvil for decision-making, the crash-out space for the tired. Never in the field of human habitation has so much been owed to one sofa by so many. Spaces and functions need to be in conversation. Researchers are strange: at times they yearn for silent individual space to delve deep, think, ponder and guess; then they want to burst into shared space to test out what they are finding. It is another example of the oscillating dynamic, called alone and together, that all communities need to embrace.

The training college reminded me of the happy years at St John's College, Nottingham, with dedicated different places in which to worship, teach, dig out books, eat, decide, be by oneself and meet others along its corridors. All this began to gain a sharper focus in 2007, when Sue Hope and I worked together within this Sheffield Campus of Church Army. Both of us were committed to the reimagination of church, of which planting fresh expressions is one fruit, and we wanted Church Army to have a significant role to play in that unfolding story. She commented that the complex we occupied contained five classic monastic places: Chapel, Cloister, Garden, Refectory and Scriptorium. We mused together to what degree the architecture, occupancy and management of our building assisted, or at times impeded, the intentions of those spaces. I thank her for crystallising what readers now know has been my very long learning process.

What did others think?

Since 2002 I had been aware of Northumbria Community, and in 2006 I took vows as a companion of that community. To the five classic monastic places, they taught me to add Cell, a private place for prayer and reading. During 2009 I wanted to research what others thought these six spaces were for, to see if there was any consensus. I led two workshops at that year's Church Army conference, which gave me feedback on what each place was for.

A month later I led a weekend retreat at Northumbria Community's mother house, Nether Springs, and I repeated the exercise. The participants reflected on their own experience and how the mother house exhibited these places. The conversations generated diversity of interpretation, but also a cluster effect, suggesting each place did have a particular role. Both groups insisted that I should add a seventh space: I had not spotted the place of deciding, called 'Chapter'. They were right; I had missed it.

Sabbatical wanderings and wonderings

Church Army kindly granted me a sabbatical in autumn 2009, during which I visited the famous Taizé. I also went to the lesser-known Cîteaux, where Abbot Robert began a reform of Benedictine life in 1098. It became the first Cistercian monastery, sending out Bernard, in 1115, to begin the monastery of Clairvaux.

I also spent several weeks living as a member of two mother-house teams, first with Northumbria Community and then with the Anglican Franciscans at Hilfield in Dorset. Both communities gave me an unvarnished exposure to the daily routines and pressures of their spiritual, human and practical life. During these periods I studied various monastic Rules to test whether these source documents contained historical evidence of the seven spaces. I also watched to see if the sites themselves bore witness to this idea. I found the functions were universal and usually expressed in the architecture.

Making the seven spaces public

From all this I wrote booklet number 43 in the 'Encounters on the Edge' series about the seven sacred spaces. It argued there was a set of classic architectural spaces, with their associated purposes. Working together they offer a fuller and deeper way for communities of Christian disciples to live and be church. That hunch had grown slowly and unevenly. The seeds had been sown through my OCU camp years, nurtured by years in community at St John's College, Nottingham, shaped by the ups and down of parish life, and developed by being within Northumbria Community and twelve years researching with Church Army.

By contrast, in some local congregations I had met thinness of community, threadbare welcome and disconnectedness of worship from life. 'Surely there is something more than this?' had been an enduring lament and a hope. Could it just be that the architectural features found in many monastic complexes, and their associated values, had something to teach the whole church?

A surprising take-up

Booklet 43 went out to our 400-plus subscribers. One of them, Canon Val Hamer, took the idea to Llandaff diocese, organising a diocesan synod day about it. Furthermore, her colleague Richard Lowndes produced a splendid further booklet and DVD which helpfully applied the learning at several levels: personal, congregational and wider community. Like me, they see that this way of thinking carries insights about being human, not just being a church community.

Less surprising has been some take-up within Northumbria Community, as one lens by which people can look at the dynamics of monastic life, even if it is in dispersed mode. Some fresh expressions of church have made it a yardstick by which to evaluate their common life. Other people have made it the template by which they reorder their buildings. I am grateful that this wide range of stories is now told in chapter 14. They show how the idea has been applied. The sheer breadth of these applications suggests there is a generic truth here. Ubiquity infers veracity.

I have spoken to varied groups about the seven spaces. It seems as though once explained, lights go on. People readily resonate with the discoveries. The idea has travelled well. The original 1,000 booklets have gone, but the demand has not gone away. We produced an updated edition in 2015, making people aware of further resources to fuel their explorations. That too is running out, and it is not well-known enough for people to get hold of. So I am delighted that BRF is willing to turn the idea into a book. Read on and enter the seven sacred spaces.

✤ 2 ✤

Enter the
seven sacred spaces

As a child of the 1950s I particularly enjoyed reading Enid Blyton's 'Adventure' series, beginning with *The Island of Adventure*, starring four children and Kiki the parrot. I found them engrossing and amusing, and they remain on a top shelf. I also liked another set of adventures undertaken by some children in a town. They met in Peter and Janet's garden shed, entered only via a strictly controlled password. They reported suspicious local goings-on and plotted responses, fortified by ginger biscuits washed down with lemonade. They were 'The Secret Seven'.

Here come a different seven, which I think have remained too secret for too long. Let the seven sacred spaces enter your thinking. Explore how you, in turn, could enter them and indeed pass through them to what lies beyond. Passwords are not needed.

I wonder why

Let's start with some questions. Why is it that houses that work well for their inhabitants usually seem to have a variety of spaces: dining rooms, gardens, cosy corners, private places, a study and welcoming reception rooms, all linked by corridors? Have you ever felt, as I have, that some smaller houses with only one downstairs lounge-diner sometimes feel claustrophobic and controlling? They don't model relaxed lounging, and the dining area takes up space only used periodically. This monospace seems to forbid diversity of people and their pursuits. Its uniformity precludes healthy diversity.

Similarly, why does the layout of some church buildings not work well as social space? In theory, they were set up for the worship of God together, but the 'together' part often feels thin. Box pews were an extreme expression of church done in separated compartments. Even with ordinary pews it is known for members of congregations to sit at the antiseptic maximum distance from one another. Some pews are not so much occupied as defended. Filing out at the end, people but nod to one another and may, or may not, shake the minster's hand.

Conversely, what complex factors contribute to the contemporary attraction of cathedrals and reports of growing numbers of visitors? Of course, there is grandeur, architectural magnificence, a sense of history and a sense of the transcendent or numinous. But is it an accident that they also encompass multiple spaces, including chapels, cloisters, chapter house and quiet corners, often set in a surrounding green space, all with various vistas to visit? And these days many have added a cafe? It seems we flourish better as humans when the spaces we occupy express and enable a diversity of functions across the unity of the overall site.

One clue that teases out responses to all those questions comes through noticing the patterns, throughout the centuries, by which parts of the Church of Christ have lived in communities of worship, study and work. These groups have lived with each other for a long time. Long-stay community is always testing: it tests resolve and relationships. Those in them had to make community and their calling work sufficiently well. These monastic communities found over time that their life together needed to be formed by agreed biblically based values, attitudes and practices, brought into a document called the Rule. These factors are truly foundational, but in turn they became linked to, and expressed in, seven distinct spaces.

The spaces, or their function, crop up within the sayings telling of the personal and communal experiences and thinking of the desert fathers and mothers. The existence of many of the spaces occurs in the Rule of Augustine (AD397). The seven can be clearly discerned in the sixth-century Rule of Benedict and those who interpret his work. They are witnessed to in various Rules written between the sixth and eighth centuries for the autonomous Celtic monastic communities. Similarly they are found in the writing and practice of the 13th-century Franciscans and their successors today.

This chapter sets out the essence of what each of the seven is about. Even as this chapter unfolds, you may well find yourself saying, 'I recognise that place; I just didn't know this technical term for it.' By all means begin linking my writing to your own experience of that space and its presence. Sometimes your reaction will be quite the opposite. You may find yourself thinking, 'I wish we had one of those spaces in my church', or you realise it is missing, devalued or distorted in wider society.

I have put the seven in alphabetical order. This is one way of trying to say that they all matter and it doesn't help, at this stage, to try to work out which may be more central or how they interact. I will make those comments about their relative priorities later. The book gives a separate chapter to each one to develop the headlines given here.

Headlines of the seven spaces

Cell is a small, secluded space where a person meets privately with God, and meets their inner self. This is the only totally private place out of the seven; all the others are shared. This feature reminds us that life in Christ is lived both *alone* as well as together. The dynamic of *together* is essential to all the other six spaces.

Chapel is the venue of public, corporate, shaped worship. This kind of worship is measured and structured; it is intentionally like that and intended to be educative. It is praise and various kinds of prayer. It is prayer with and for others. Chapel operates in rhythms and regularity. These create a familiarity to be passed through, not to get stuck at or bored by. In the period of Christendom, 'church' too often shrunk down to only the Chapel function. I show that this is an error, and I offer a richer understanding.

Chapter is the building where a community makes decisions about its life together. Here leaders and members communicate, discuss, debate and disagree, in order to decide. Historically, each monastic member was accountable to the others in the chapter. It was called a chapter because either verses from scripture or part of the order's rule was read. It reminded the decision-makers that everyone sits under authority. They are to listen to others with due attention. They need to resist temptations to condemn or dismiss others.

Cloister makes connections. Its feature was sheltered walkways and corridors that linked up the other places, so people walked up and down them. They also sat and inhabited them. Monks used this space to change gear, such as the shift from eating to attending worship. Cloister therefore is the place of planned and surprising encounters. You may meet the person you are trying to avoid. But to bump into a beloved friend, whom you have not seen in a while, will be a joy. How we talk with everyone as we negotiate the cloister, whether they are friends or a person we find difficult, is an aspect of community that always matters.

Garden is not about idyllic rest and the beauty of nature; rather, it stands for the place of fruitful work. Originally the garden of the monastery provided food for the table of the community. Its spiritual function also gave a balance to the other two areas of godly work done by monks, namely prayer and study. God has made us in his image, which includes being creative and creatures who work. Without any work, life lacks meaning; conversely doing good work is deeply satisfying. Work guards us against idleness, making it a friend to the soul. But it is not the place of quick results.

Refectory is the eating place. It beats at the heart of community and nourishes it. That is true both literally and socially. Families and communities express their oneness by eating together. This dynamic also works the other way round. Those we regularly eat with, we become one with. Refectory also extends community by providing hospitality. The words eating, meeting and greeting sound alike and are connected. When people eat together, they begin to belong. It is a place of both work and rest.

Scriptorium is another of three classic places of monastic work. Originally it was more about learning to pass on knowledge than simply acquiring it for its own sake. Scribes handwrote the only books that existed. They wrote to enable others to have books to learn from and from which to say their prayers. The kind of learning it fosters matters too. Slow, thoughtful, spiritual learning is about transformation of the heart, not mainly about information for the head. In Christianity, love trumps knowledge, as 1 Corinthians 13 reminds us. This type of learning is all about becoming more like Christ and his virtues.

What this book covers

Some of the chapters that follow open wider issues connected to the seven spaces as a whole, while others delve into detail about each of the seven spaces.

Chapters 3 to 9 go into detail about each of the spaces in turn. I have attempted to distil the comments and wisdom on them, which I have gathered from three sources:

1 within the monastic writers themselves and later commentators
2 current groups exploring the idea of these spaces
3 my own observation of the architecture and dynamics within classic and contemporary monastic communities that I have visited or worked in.

Chapter 10 asks why we should learn from monasticism at all, bearing in mind its danger of elitism and historical corruption and its disappearance in the Protestant Church at the Reformation. This chapter also tracks the rise and character of so-called new monasticism and explores the role of the monastic in relation to society and in the renewing purposes of God.

Chapter 11 shows how the seven spaces can still be found and how they work out in everyday life. Anyone can still find these spaces in older university colleges, cathedrals, conference centres and bigger traditional houses. Some spaces have lost their prominence, as priorities between them have changed, but the overall inheritance remains. I suspect the seven spaces embody functions that turn out to be part of being fully human. Part of their value is that they offer one way to assess what it is to be human and how we are intended to live together. Yet in secular use the balance across them has been changed, as has the way they are understood and applied. This chapter also critiques a dominant view of church life which has overinvested in Chapel.

Chapter 12 picks up the relationship of the seven sacred spaces to the topic of mission. It has to face the concern that the spaces are too inward-looking and that they appear to deal exclusively with relationships within the Christian community. Can and do they travel outwards?

Then chapter 13 investigates what connections there are to discipleship. This is a topic of renewed interest recently. But this occurs at a time in which our understanding of discipleship, in my view, is changing for the better. The seven spaces have a voice to be heard in that conversation.

Chapter 14 is stories. In their own words eight people talk about how the seven spaces approach has affected their lives, homes, groups, churches and even a diocese.

The final chapter tries to be frank about what the seven spaces cannot do and be modest about what they can do. For example, one unhelpful approach is to try to impose them. A variety of different images are explored for how they do work and how we can cooperate with them. I explore them seen as a diet, a language, a lens, a ring road and a portal. All these images offer insights into these possibilities and limitations, mixing realism and hope.

I'll be candid. Thinking in terms of the seven sacred spaces is not a magic formula to solve everything. However, it can act in a diagnostic way to spot the strengths and weaknesses in our private lives, our homes, our churches and our local communities. As we see more clearly by what means communities work well, we have a better chance to live richer lives and to create sustainable, healthy churches. This can occur because we have learnt these lessons from the past, and as we grow into the patterns of shared life which God the Holy Trinity always had for us.

Different sources, contexts, emphases

It would be tedious in each of chapters 3–9 to explain why the evidence from the primary source – the monastic texts – is uneven, so I unpack it here. I have spent days on end trying to read carefully through various Rules and sayings that come from different sources: the Desert Fathers, Augustinian, Benedictine, Celtic and Franciscan. I have also read commentators on these different strands. I am painfully aware that I am no expert in any of them and only sense something of their wisdom and diversity of approach. I am also grateful that I have lived for over 15 years in one Celtic strand of new monasticism, as a companion within Northumbria Community. Whether that creates a bias, others must judge. If this dive into these monastic deeper waters is not for you, turn to the end of this chapter, where you can pray the prayer you will find there.

Treasures from the desert

A key source is John Cassian (AD360–435) from what is modern-day Romania. He initially only visited the desert monasteries, first in Palestine and then in Egypt, but eventually stayed from c. 385–399. Travelling west over the years, in 415 he set up two monasteries in Marseilles. Around 420–425 he wrote up a distillation of desert teaching, codifying their sayings, in two collections called *The Institutes* and *The Conferences of the Fathers*.[1] Both collections major on the eight vices that afflict the soul and their opposite virtues, which bring healing, and on the life of prayer leading to true contemplation. Hence their focus appears to be the inner life, fought out in Cell, which is named in the often-cited saying from Abba Moses: 'Go to your Cell, for your Cell will teach you everything.' Yet their wider sayings clearly address community relations and the need to renounce judging others, either in our thoughts or at meetings that look like Chapter.[2] They also commended consistent commitment to work (Garden) in basket weaving, the demands of hospitality (Refectory) and shared worship (Chapel).

Cassian is a major source for the spiritual dynamics demonstrated in several later strands. Benedict, in his Rule, recommends his work is read to the community (42.3, 73.5).[3] Contemporary Benedictine writers, such as Sister Meg Funk, focus on this path to Christlikeness by contending with the eight vices, which she calls 'afflictions'.[4] Cassian's approach lies behind the approach taken by the various Irish Celtic Rules and also the Celtic penitentials that I comment on later. From him, I take that the mental battle of living a life in Christ, alone and together, is central. The spaces are but the arenas in which that life is played out.

Hints from Augustine

Augustine wrote his Rule in 397 for the lay community gathered around the bishop's house in Hippo, but before he became its bishop. It is thought to be the oldest in the western church. It is short, with eight chapters and 48 subsections, barely taking up five A4 pages. It begins and ends with motives and attitudes: the start is the gospel call to 'love God and then your neighbour', and the end is an injunction to 'observe all these precepts in a spirit of charity, as lovers of spiritual beauty... living... as men and women living in freedom under grace'. Augustine's focus on love and beauty reflects his experience and conviction that the heart of Christian living is to be captivated by a delight in God. That delight is God's gift by the Holy Spirit: 'God's love has been poured into our hearts through the Holy Spirit, who has been given to us' (Romans 5:5).[5] And all true love is a delight. I unpack this approach in chapter 3 on Cell.

Minimalist rules emphasise attitudes and deal less with practice or place. This one addresses tensions that could arise in a mixed community made of those from rich backgrounds and poor ones and of both the healthy and the weak, the principle being 'they had all things in common and each was given what he needed' (1.4), even if this meant different treatment being offered and resources shared unequally. The two 'afflictions' most addressed are pride and lust, unsurprisingly for Augustine, with the latter approached, as in the sermon on the mount, as an issue for the eyes and the heart.

The Rule was taken up more widely in the 12th and 13th centuries, not least by a group called the Augustinians, or White Friars, of whom later Luther was one, and by the Dominicans, the Black Friars. Both orders were seeking to engage with and preach to a society becoming increasingly urban and moving away from the rural estates familiar in Benedict's time; it was growing in literacy and with shifts of mercantile wealth and power. Augustine's Rule was more ascetic, and thus countercultural, than the Rule of Benedict.

What does it demonstrate about the spaces? Some are explicit; others are implied. We are told there was an oratory and free time to pray (Chapel; 2.10–11 and 4.24) and that they ate together and listened to readings (Refectory; 2.15). There was work done for the community (Garden; 5.31) and in the reading of books (Scriptorium;

5.38 and 5.39). Uncorrected faults could come to a common meeting (Chapter; 4.27). Clearly they met socially and across differences of station in life, so the dangers of quarrelling, anger and forgiveness are covered (Cloister; 6.41–42). Most functions, except Cell, and appropriate attitudes are there, if not the names. Unlike some other monastic groups, they were neither enclosed nor forbidden to go beyond their buildings (4.20 and 5.36), but they were to go in groups.

The core role of the Rule of Benedict

Attempts to summarise the approach and contribution of the Rule of Benedict feel like trying to catch a waterfall in a teacup. It is far longer than Augustine's, at 73 chapters, with far more detail about monastic community life. Its fame is partly due to the fact that it and its communities are credited with saving Christian Europe in the Dark Ages.[6] Esther De Waal also sees it as striking a balance between Cassian's ascetic desert sources and the more humane communal Rule of St Basil.[7] But the Rule is modest about itself, commending both these loftier sources as 'tools for the cultivation of virtues' (73.6) and describing itself as 'written for beginners' (73.8).

The aim and character of the Rule is spelt out in the Prologue (P). It comes from Benedict as a loving father (P.1), explaining that the Lord is calling the monks to this way of life, striking a balance between the obedience of doing good deeds (P.22) and the fact that 'it is the Lord's power not their own that brings about the good in them' (P.29). The tools for this are the love of Christ and of others (4.21). It is 'to establish a school for the Lord's service' (P.45), in which there is 'nothing harsh, nothing burdensome' (P.46). So Benedict counsels, 'Do not be daunted immediately by fear and run away from the road that leads to salvation' (P.48). The Rule is full of scriptural quotations. 'It is an immersion in the Gospel life so intense that we never forget for a moment what we are about.'[8]

Benedict is a keen observer of human nature, and the Rule is humane, at points almost humorous. Its people can't match the worship accomplishments of the Fathers (18.25), the sleepy like to make excuses (22.8), they need a spiritual doctor (27.1) and they may be weak (34:2). Extra work needs extra food (35.12); people get sick (36.1-9) and need different diets (39.1). They can be late – God forbid (11.12) – or miss chapel and go back to bed (43.8). They can be needy (55.21) and find a task impossible (68:1-5). The abbot must be aware of his own frailty (64.13) and amend his own faults (2.40). Therefore 'he should so regulate and arrange all matters that souls may be saved and the brothers go about their activities without justifiable grumbling' (41.5).

There is also respect for context. Benedict makes allowance for flexible practice, even in worship, in the face of the seasons of the year, the age and strength of monks and the effect of weather. The same applies to discipline. The abbot acts with 'discretion, the mother of virtues… that the strong have something to yearn for and the weak have nothing to run from' (64.19). 'Coaxing, reproving and encouraging them as appropriate, he must so accommodate and adapt himself to each one's character and intelligence' (2.31–32). Even joining the community is a genuinely free choice. In the year of the novitiate, the Rule is read to potential newcomers on three separate occasions. If they choose to submit to it, it is because it was something they were 'free either to reject or to accept' (58.16). Moreover, those brothers who later either choose or are made to leave the monastery may be readmitted up to three times (29.1–3).

Knowing what people are like means that the Rule deals in the practicalities of many things: the rhythms of the day across worship, study and work, down to food, clothing and bedding. It deals with decision-making, discipline, guests and requests to join the community.

In view of all this attention to practical and communal detail, and because the monasteries were built to be self-sufficient (66.6), it is not surprising that nearly all the seven spaces, or what they are for, are named, with several chapters specifically on Chapel and others on Refectory. Cloister is not named as such, but so much comment is made on the communal life of the monastery that it is impossible to think its function did not exist, and all Benedictine monasteries that I know have actual cloisters. The Rule of Benedict is the major historical source which has undergirded my thinking.

Catching Celtic voices

If working with Benedict is like standing under a waterfall, catching the Celtic contribution is more like trying to herd wild geese, as it is made up of several autonomous sources rather than one dominant rule. All seven places are not named in many of these diverse Celtic Rules. For example, in the six pages of the Rule of Columbanus the only suggestions of the places are the comment at the end of chapter 3, 'Every day we must pray, labour and read,' and the phrases 'each should pray in his cell' and 'the depth of his study' in chapter 7. The Rules are much more interested in combating spiritual vices and cultivating spiritual virtues.[9]

To find liberation from the vices was a process through sin, sorrow, penance and health, for which the Celtic penitentials were penned. These documents take Cassian's view that penance is a form of healing, not of punishment. It assists the growth of the virtue which opposes a vice. The giver of the penance is like a spiritual GP prescribing a course of medicine, but for the medicine to work the sick person must take it. The Penitential of Cummean describes itself as 'the medicine for the salvation of souls'. It has Cassian's eight spiritual illnesses and draws on the medical views of the time: 'The eight principal vices contrary to human salvation shall be healed by the eight remedies that are their contraries' (Cummean 14). From the nature of the penances imposed, we can deduce the functions of many of the seven spaces, but they are not named.

Hard evidence for the seven spaces comes from writers about Celtic monasticism. Uinseann Ó Maidín explains that they followed the pattern of secular habitation. The ring fort was one to three rings of earth with the living quarters inside. The buildings inside were made from timber or wattle and daub, which were never going to last long. Space between the rings was for animals and vegetable gardens. From him we know of four distinct places:

> The inner enclosure therefore provided the space in which the principal buildings of the monastery were to be found; a church of no great proportions, the cells of the monks, the guest house and the refectory.[10]

Cardinal Tomás Ó Fiaich wrote about Columbanus (543–615) in *Columbanus in His Own Words* and describes Bangor monastery in Ireland, where Columbanus spent his youth.[11] He concurs with Ó Maidín that as well as a garden area, there were shared wooden cells and communal buildings: the church, refectory and guesthouse. Monks in Bangor learnt Latin and some Greek, read the pagan classical authors and knew the scriptures intimately. Those with the talent spent time copying manuscripts, so Scriptorium is there too. Five spaces can be deduced, plus the guesthouse, which I see as an extension of the hospitality function. Thomas Cahill, an American historian, in his *How the Irish Saved Civilisation*, concurs:

> Irish monks preferred to spend their time in study, prayer, farming – and, of course, copying. So the basic plan of the monastery was quickly executed: a little hut for each monk... a refectory and kitchen; a scriptorium and library; a smithy, a kiln, a mill and a couple of barns; a modest church – and they were in business.[12]

He too witnesses to five out of the seven places, with various workplaces doing duty for garden. Cloister and Chapter are missing as named features, but there were pathways between the other places, so Cloister is not absent.

The Rule of Ailbe is an eight-century text, attributed out of reverence to Ailbe, who died in 534.[13] It is different in that it is in 66 metrical verses so that it might be more easily remembered. Yet it is very practical – it names Cell, Refectory and Chapel and has much to say on attitudes that apply to all the seven spaces. Across these disparate Celtic documents I have found that the beloved triad, of prayer, labour and study, is echoed in many Rules.[14] These three central roles lead us to Cell and Chapel, to Garden and Scriptorium. We know too that they ate and met and had to handle discipline. All seven are there if we look with care.

The Franciscan adventure

I went for the word 'adventure' in the heading to this section, because encountering Francis is meeting a passion and quest rather than a plan or procedures.[15] The image I have of trying to summarise his connection to the seven spaces is the futility of trying to bottle the wind. His passion was living in response to the visionary call of Jesus and living out the spirit and simple life of Jesus. As such he had no interest in the seven spaces themselves, and the acquisition of property was vigorously resisted.

Nevertheless, a Franciscan Rule emerged, but in stages. The first Rule, now all but lost, was written c. 1209, by which time there were twelve brothers.[16] At that stage there was 'as yet no organization, no cloister, and no Rule beyond the simple words of the Gospel'.[17] It was based around three texts that Francis found, as became his habit, by 'opening the Bible at random, expecting to find God's guidance in the word of scripture'[18] – Matthew 19:21 ('sell your possessions and give to the poor'); Luke 9:3 ('take nothing for the journey'); and Matthew 16:24 ('whoever wants to be my disciple must deny themselves and take up their cross and follow me'). It was only informally approved.

The second Rule, which was not approved, hence being called the *Regula non bullata*, was composed in 1219 and is 24 chapters long. It expanded the 1209 version to respond to questions of conduct that had arisen. How should the friars worship if, through absolute poverty, they had no churches to pray in or books to pray from?

Equally, what should they do with the few properties that were given to them? How should they both eat and fast? Should they balance working for a living and asking for alms? How was the preaching that had now been happening for over a decade to be done?[19] How was it to be balanced by contemplation? How should they make decisions in chapter and regulate the groups of Franciscans now starting up in other European countries?

In 1222 Francis drafted the so-called Second Rule with Cardinal Ugolino (later Pope Gregory IX), who acted as cardinal-protector to the young order and persuaded Francis to tone down some parts that would have caused conflict with the wider church. It was discussed by the Society of Saint Francis chapter in June 1223 and confirmed by Pope Honorious III the following November.[20] It is a third of the textual length of the 1219 version and only twelve chapters.

In this shorter, approved 1223 Rule, there is little to nothing about the spaces Franciscans occupied. This is for several reasons. First, 'Francis did not produce a system, but lived a life.' His life was of divine visitations that called him to conversion to Christ and growing into Christlikeness. It was dynamic, not systematic; he was a man of 'spontaneity and uninhibited emotional freedom'.[21] Second, there was the passionate belief in the renunciation of all possessions, including at that stage owning any community property.[22] Latterly it was given to them and not refused. Third, the brothers were intended to live not so much in, as out of, their simple communal life in a friary. Their life pattern enabled by alms was praying, wandering and preaching: 'The Franciscan cloister was the world.'[23] Fourth, the early communities were so small as to merge all these functions. We know of Francis' instructions about this in *Religious Life in Hermitages*: 'Not more than three or at most four friars should go together to a hermitage to lead a religious life there.'[24] Finally, 'Francis had no taste for book learning and was always suspicious about scholarship with the Order.'[25] In addition study would mean cost, time and buildings in which to keep books and the materials to make them.

Francis' attitude is perhaps best summarised in his own words, bearing in mind the corruption and laxity by then within the older orders.

> My brothers, God called me to walk in the way of humility and showed me the way of simplicity. I do not want to hear any mention of the rule of St Augustine, of St Bernard or of St Benedict. The Lord has told me that he wanted to make a new fool of me in the world, and God does not want to lead us by any other knowledge than that.[26]

Yet by the end of the 13th century, it is estimated there were 30,000 friars, and a process of standardisation had occurred. Two streams of Franciscan life had emerged, even in the later years of Francis' life, against his vision: the *Spirituals* – or zealous ones – followed his teaching about poverty literally; the *Conventuals* – or relaxed ones – would own communal property. Harsh words, like 'fanatics' and 'compromisers', were bandied about. Schism sadly followed, and they are now separate Roman Catholic families. Yet it is the practices of the latter group that give us access to Franciscan use of the seven spaces.

Today, these founding documents are supplemented by a contemporary document called *The Principles of the First Order*, with the 1223 Rule seen as a founding document but not closely applied. It is found in *The Daily Office SSF*, the Anglican Franciscan version of *Celebrating Common Prayer*,[27] in the form of daily readings across a month, including the characteristic three notes of the order – humility, love and joy. In addition, there is agreement that the Franciscan way is different to other orders, because 'the Franciscan past is very strongly personalised… It consists in the experience of a man and his companions, more than legislative or narrative texts.'[28]

The Principles of the First Order is historically and textually dependent on a prototypical Anglican Indian Rule of 1934[29] and offers connections to the spaces. The communities 'live as a family having all things in common' and in buildings which are 'the simplest that are consistent with good health and efficient work'.[30] I cite the connections in chapters 3–9. The Anglican SSF mother house, Hilfield Friary in Dorset, which opened in 1921, exhibits all the seven spaces, as does the later northern equivalent at Alnmouth, opened in the 1960s.

Thus the text of the Rule is more about principles than regulations, and Francis the founder is the magnetic force. Hence there are ceaseless biographies about him. Some readers may know the novel *Chasing Francis*, in which a burnt-out American pastor finds renewed and deeper spiritual life by encounter with the Franciscan adventure.[31]

Francis is a timely reminder that more is at stake here than the existence of the seven spaces or even their functions. Still less should we be fussed about being keen to actually build them. That would be to repeat Francis' own error in 1209 to literally 'rebuild my church, which is in ruins'. No, this rebuilding is the rediscovery of life in Christ, met by him, transformed by him. The seven spaces might, at best, be portals to that life; they are not the life itself. Yet they occur with such consistency across the monastic tradition that we are wise to heed them.

Testing the seven sacred spaces idea

I've wanted to be honest and open about whether my first source of information – the monastic texts – does truly support my belief that the seven spaces matter. You will have seen that across these sources they are unevenly referred to, either directly by name or indirectly by mentioning what I have come to think of as their function. In those senses I am satisfied that they are present. Cell, Chapel and Refectory are named most often, perhaps Cloister the least. However, it is also clear that the spiritual and mental roles they play are far more important than the actual place. Moreover, the more mobile the monastic order and its rule, the greater the emphasis on what the spaces assist, rather than on having buildings to support them. That turns out to be helpful, for few of us will live in actual monasteries, nor have the leisure or resources to build one.

Go through the portal

If the seven sacred spaces can act as a portal, as the subtitle of this book has it, then you might care to pray this prayer (the Anglican collect for the Fourth Sunday after Trinity), which models the need to pass through the external architectural shapes of the spaces to get to what is of greater spiritual value beyond them:

O God, the protector of all that trust in thee,
without whom nothing is strong, nothing is holy:
Increase and multiply upon us thy mercy;
that, thou being our ruler and guide,
we may so pass through things temporal,
that we finally lose not the things eternal:
Grant this, O heavenly Father, for Jesus Christ's sake our Lord.

✛ 3 ✛

CELL

being alone with God

What sort of Cell?

For any who skipped bits of chapter 2 and dived in here, I need to clarify what Cell is not.

It does not mean a locked small room in a prison, except that those too can be places of reflection, realisation and repentance. Monastic cells are entered voluntarily, and you hold any keys.

Nor is Cell about the small building-blocks in the biology of living things, although the issue of what makes for life does occur in both, and Cell is the smallest place of the seven.

Nor is Cell to do with what some call 'cell church', a way of being church that is based on small groups that are highly intentional about discipleship and evangelism and grow by reproducing further ones. This expression of church was brought to the UK in 1995 from the Far East, and there are still some churches in the UK based on that thinking, as well as literature about how to start and sustain them. Both are about going further with God, but there the similarity ends.

In this book, by Cell I mean the small space, wherever it is, in which a person meets privately with God and thereby meets their inner self.

The foundation that is Cell

Up till now I have not assigned any priority across the seven sacred spaces. Yet the more I have read and thought about Cell, the more I am convinced that it is crucial among the seven and makes some claim to priority because of its foundational history and spiritual role.

That foundational history begins in the monastic tradition that was started by Anthony of Egypt (251–356) and just with Cell. Only as groups of cells gathered did communal monastic life evolve. When it comes to role, Cell has long been seen as foundational in that it is the prime place for confronting oneself and one's 'demons' and thereby growing, dependent on God and in the grace of spiritual disciplines.

> A certain brother came to the abbot Moses seeking a word from him. And the old man said to him: 'Go sit in your cell, and your cell will teach you everything'... Anthony of Egypt explains why: 'The one who sits in solitude and quiet has escaped from three wars: hearing, speaking and seeing; yet against one thing shall he continually battle: that is, his own heart.'[1]

It is hard to top that sentence – 'Your cell will teach you everything.' Its subsequent width of use in history is shown that in the west, Cell was notably practised by Martin, outside Tours. Probably it came to Celtic Christianity through Ninian, who visited Martin. It continued in all subsequent monastic orders. In the east, Cell has been expressed either in sole occupancy of desert dwellings for hermits or through the *poustinia* – Russian for desert – the place occupied by a *staretz* or holy person.

I have become convinced that a Christian cannot grow, mature and deepen in following Christ, becoming more like him, without the spiritual foundational work that is undertaken principally in the space called Cell. What occurs in the other six spaces of communal life may well then test the spiritual progress made in the Cell.

An image of that relationship is that the six other spaces are like the walls and roof built upon this foundation. If the foundation is not sound, cracks will appear higher up and the structure may fall down. Yet the relationship is also dynamic. The proper need for substantial walls may test the adequacy of the foundations. The other spaces will reveal what issues of spiritual and personal development still need to be faced up to in Cell. For example, living with that annoying person in community will show how far I have mastered my own feelings of anger. The privileges given to others, or their abilities, will show me how well I cope with my own pride, avarice or envy.

What is the evidence for Cell and its roles?

I know 'Cell' is not a word that occurs in the Bible, but then neither is 'Trinity'. However, one biblical root is in Jesus' command in Matthew 6:6: 'But when you pray, go into your room, close the door and pray to your Father, who is unseen.' That teaching is buttressed by Jesus' example of taking private time with God, notably before making big decisions, before choosing the twelve disciples, when confronted with misunderstood popularity and when in Gethsemane. He showed that going to the cell is an instinct, which might use a variety of private or secret spaces.

These could overlap with the other six spaces. For a person who meets God in the delights of nature, practising cell might be outdoors, a link to Garden. For those who come alive through reading, Cell meets Scriptorium. Those helped by magnificent buildings with ritual and symbol are mixing Cell and Chapel. Those who are drawn to care for others may find Cell and Refectory overlap. Ascetics and contemplatives are likely to gravitate to a classic solitary cell.[2]

Cell in the various Rules

The Rule of Benedict

The Rule of Benedict seems not to know of the Cell, but rather has the monks living in dormitories. It speaks of them being in separate beds, ideally all in one place (22.1). However, with larger communities, they slept in supervised dormitories of 10 or 20 monks (22.3). This occurred at a time when, among the rural poor, living in one room and having a communal bed was common. Thus Benedict balances some privacy with simplicity. Commentators see this practice as emphasising community, living the common life, in contrast to today's individualism and insistence on personal space, and where many bedrooms are further individualised by being en suite. The practice of dormitories is now long discontinued, and monks sleep, rest, pray, study and read in their own room.

Yet the Rule and Benedictine commentators make much of the values Cell espouses. The Rule urges 'esteem for silence' (6.2), and Chittister warns of the danger of living in a 'century saturated with information', filled with the 'static of nonsense' and a 'noise-polluted world'.[3] Commenting on the power of silence, Abbot Jamison knows the Carthusian call to the contemplative life is only for some, but adds, 'It must fill some of life for all people.'[4] So he points to where the Rule says, 'The disciple is to be silent and listen' (6.6).[5]

However, because it is also the place to confront one's demons, silence and Cell do not lead to tranquillity, but rather identification of trouble and of battles ahead. In that spirit, Chittister cites Abba Agathon: 'There is no labour greater than that of prayer to God... Prayer is warfare to the last breath.'[6] Yet despite this struggle, Benedict does not think prayer should be wordy:

> We must know that God regards our purity of heart and tears of compunction[7] not our many words. Prayer should therefore be short and pure unless perhaps it is prolonged under the inspiration of divine grace. (20.4)

It is also clear from the Rule (9.10; 10.2; 12.4 and 13.11) that many key passages used in worship are to be learnt by heart (books were not plentiful), and Cell would have been one space in which such familiarity could be acquired (8.3).

Celtic voices

Irish Celtic evidence for Cell or its functions comes from a variety of Rules. The Rule of Ailbe (see pages 39-40) has four citations which show the purposes and evidence the location: 'Let him be gentle in his vigils and like a fortress in his prayer'; 'The son of God should be invoked in all *lectio*'; 'Let prayer be the support of each one as he watches in his cell'; and 'Be faithful to prayer in your cell.'[8]

The shorter Rule of Comgall focuses on the spiritual battle, without naming Cell, for example: 'When faced with innumerable battles against many vices, against the devil, or against the body, it is essential that you be resolute.' Elsewhere it is explicit about the eight vices and eight virtues to combat them.[9] The ninth-century Rule of Carthage urges that 'we watch, we read, we pray' and 'after the meal let each return to his cell where he is to read, pray and importune the King (God)'.[10] The earlier Rule of Columbanus (543–615) explicitly says that 'each should pray in his own cell' and has a whole section on 'mortification', or dying to oneself.[11]

Clearly this was a serious matter that needed both regulation and encouragement, for elsewhere we find: 'We watch, we read, we pray, each of us according to our strength.'[12] But by contrast very tough words exist: 'Prayer should be until tears come' (the ninth-century so-called Rule of Colmcille, 27). An early Irish poem called 'The Scribe in the Woods' touches a number of these aspects, including living with the reality of death:

All alone in my little Cell, without the company of anyone;
precious has been the pilgrimage before going to meet death.
A hidden secluded little hut, for the forgiveness of my sins:
an upright untroubled conscience towards holy heaven.

Sanctifying the body be good habits, trampling like a man upon it;
with weak and tearful eyes for the forgiveness of my passions...
All alone in my little cell, all alone thus:
Alone I came into the world, alone I shall go from it.

Franciscan sources

Turning to the Franciscan voice, there is little to nothing about the seven spaces in the first short approved 1223 Rule, because Francis held to literal poverty and early Franciscan friaries were only of a few people. It covers their calling for Christ-centred devotion, testing the call, the balance of work and prayer, avoidance of learning and issues of discipline. Simplicity was all. As mentioned in chapter 2, I draw from a more recent Franciscan document, *The Principles of the First Order*, which does offer connections. Contemporary evidence comes from the layout of Anglican Franciscan houses, such as Hilfield Friary in Dorset and Alnmouth in Northumberland. They exhibit all the seven features, including Cell.

Texts that bear upon Cell include 'Principles' day 8, advising that friars are to conquer temptations and practise faithful self-discipline. Day 17 covers private prayer, which is to be safeguarded, with the perceptive comment that corporate worship is not a substitute for it. The aim is continual prayer affecting the whole of life. I know Hilfield reasonably well, having lived there for several weeks on sabbatical. Each Hilfield brother has his own room, as do the guests. Francis himself adds a crucial factor and a typically radical and missional Franciscan note: 'Wherever we are, or wherever we go, we always take our cell with us; for Brother Body is our cell, and our soul is the hermit who lives in it.'[13]

Ultimately Cell is more than a location; it is an interior reality, which having a place fortifies. It is an indispensable foundation among the seven spaces, evidenced from a range of monastic writings, and thus primary in any Christian life serious about following Jesus.

Cell seen by the focus groups

Those at the Church Army workshops saw a linked group of purposes: 'Private space, retreat, personal relationship with God and oneself, inner work, spiritual battleground, place of meditation, reflecting on listening to the community and to the world, time to read, to write, to sleep.' Meg Funk OSB pushes the sleep aspect further: 'It is a place to sleep, to surrender, to experience the night.' She even calls it 'a sacred space' and one in which to resist the temptation to overwork.[14]

On the Northumbria Community retreat, members concurred, using overlapping terms and purposes. They described it as 'you and God, your own place, retreat and renewal, spiritual disciplines, struggle, challenge, admission of need, a place to grow'. The practice of it included silence and solitude, peace, listening, isolation, being cut off, escaping, bringing the world to God in intercession. They too included the important function of sleep, adding the role of dreams. They thought Cell needed to be in one's own room – a familiar, daily place with no distractions – though some laughed and cited Susanna Wesley (mother of John) praying in her kitchen with her apron over her head. Ideally it was quiet, being alone with, attending to and chatting with God. It was a space for the inner journey, one of increased expectation, adoration and self-examination, letting God speak and allowing God to come, making space for God to deal with us; a place to journal and do *lectio divina*, not study.

Contemporary experience

The present expression of Cell in mother houses and intentional communities is usually the bedroom, though it can be another dedicated quiet corner. What is characteristic is that it is occupied daily; it is familiar private yet simple space. As such, it is different from, and complementary to, all the other six spaces, which are busier. Today using a bedroom is normal, because although some retreat centres also have a *poustinia*, a tiny, unheated, unlit, bare room in the grounds, this is not recommended for daily winter use, and the monastic journey with God is undoubtedly a daily one.

Clarity about its purpose may not be matched by frequency in its practice. David, a vicar friend, serving a local church and working through the seven spaces with a parish group found:

> Despite a number of the participants having an evangelical background, and therefore discipled with a great emphasis on the 'quiet time', the reality is that most of those present have a neglected cell. They rarely manage a prayerful time alone with God and even less likely a time of silence and stillness. They survive spiritually on what happens in chapel and elsewhere. Indeed, some participants found cell way too uncomfortable.

He contrasted that void with the role and necessity of Cell as seen by Henri Nouwen, who taught that the spiritual journey includes the death to the false self, formed by external pressures and expectations, and the growth of the new self, formed by engagement with Jesus Christ:

> The secular or false self is the self which is fabricated, as Thomas Merton says, by social compulsions... It points to the need for ongoing and increasing affirmation. Who am I? I am the one who is liked, praised, admired, disliked, hated or despised... What matters is how I am perceived by my world. If being busy is a good thing, then I must be busy...
>
> In solitude I get rid of my scaffolding: no friends to talk with, no telephone calls to make, no meetings to attend, no music to entertain, no books to distract, just me... Thus I try again to run from the dark abyss of my nothingness and restore my false self in all its vainglory... That is the struggle... to die to the false self.[15]

I consider that Cell is central to counter contemporary compulsions of self-centredness and consumerism, or the vices and temptations that Nouwen names. Without entering the practice of Cell we cannot emerge spiritually healthy; 'solitude is the furnace of transformation'.[16] Such themes are echoed by the Rules, noticed by the focus groups and spotted in contemporary experience.

I realise this conflicts with my observation of being a grandparent. How parents of under-fives do Cell, I struggle to know. Perhaps snatched moments last thing at night, on the walk to the school gates or being alone in the bathroom is realism. Respite care on a retreat would be welcome, too. Mind you, often the public worship of Chapel isn't much of a haven for these parents either.

Why Cell is different to all the other six places

There is something fundamentally valuable about being alone. Being alone is often confused with concepts like loneliness and being an individual. Those last two connect. Loneliness might be called the unwelcome absence of others, whereas being alone can be the pleasure and adventure of solitude. Rowan Williams helpfully distinguishes between the terms 'individual' and 'person'. Being an individual is a way of being a particular example – just a differentiated example of humankind. By contrast, being a person is 'the unique intersection of the relationships in which it is involved'.[17] We are persons because of others. Note that we never speak of the three 'individuals' of the Trinity and have been rightly taught to call them persons. They are persons in community, though their being 'three in one' goes beyond even our minds at full stretch.

In a noisy, urbanised culture scampering away from the fear of loneliness, it is countercultural to stress the necessity of being alone. In Northumbria Community there is conscious dependence on the Desert tradition, and the phrase 'Your cell will teach you everything' is often used. It is not so much what you would do in your cell, as what it would do to you. Silence, solitude and the desert are interwoven themes that are common currency in monasticism.

Nouwen remarks, 'Without solitude it is virtually impossible to live a spiritual life.'[18] Here is the insistence that each person needs to take responsibility for their own spiritual life. Neither the rule, nor the community, nor its corporate worship can deliver what Cell will expose.

Andrew Roberts' book *Holy Habits*[19] covers ten spiritual disciplines he sees within Acts 2:42–47. He names prayer as a corporate habit of the early church. The Bible Reading Fellowship has since, with him, published a set of books, one for each habit, for group use over a two-year period in order that each habit may be formed, not merely discussed. It is admirable that this level of intentionality and change of practice is being advocated. Of course, this Acts text was not intended to describe the private prayer life of the Christian, but my present understanding is that the Cell space reminds us that even Christian disciplines practised *together* will not, and in the end cannot, do the work that Cell, *alone*, must do. Yes, the other six are the proving ground of work done in Cell on character. The community throws up aspects where we need to grow as persons within it: how being with others and their curious habits is vexing, how deciding together is difficult, how work can be tedious or disagreeable. It may be true to say that through the other six we can be transformed by circumstances. In Cell we are transformed by choice.

This is of cardinal importance if today's Christians are to recover from the viruses of consumerism and dependency that are rife in church life and have crossed almost unnoticed from the deeply addictive western culture in which we live. We are conditioned to more, not less. We prefer provision on the shelf, not surprising finds in strange places. We are used to opening a package, not creating it ourselves. Cell may be what we most flee from, for it will strip us of pretence, our glib second-hand opinions, our preference for experts to top up our spiritual bank balance and most dreadfully it will show us ourselves. But this is the doorway to truer liberation in Christ. As such, the desert is a place not of escapism but rather of stark reality. As Williams put it, 'In the desert the insoluble problem is myself.'[20] Cell is the address for finding our own vulnerability and being vulnerable to God.

I suggest it goes beyond the 'quiet time' of the evangelical tradition. Positively that time offered rhythms of exposure to scripture, but it could slide off into being educational about scripture, not entry into the experience beyond the text. Having more information is always easier than accepting transformation. It was also weaker in exploring width or depth in prayer; it barely knew silence or contemplation, though it fostered intercession. It tended to be active and talkative.

Cell, because it is bare but for a Bible, is a place for memorising and for listening. Funk concurs: 'It is a place for listening... Rest happens and a deeper listening from the heart is restored.'[21] It reminds me of a remark by a therapist on a slimming programme on TV for grossly overweight people: 'You must learn to take food to nurture your body not blank out your mind.' Listening to God in solitude is far from the inflated diet of information fed to us by the secular and the Christian world.

Another connection comes from what the gospel stories assume to be desirable and normal in all good servants – an attitude of 'to hear is to obey'.[22] I was fascinated to discover the view of Nouwen that the linguistic root of the prime monastic word 'obedience' is the Latin *audire*, to listen.[23] Obedience, availability and aloneness are connected. We cannot be available if we will not listen. We cannot listen if we will not be attentive. We cannot attend unless we enter silence.

A pair of hints on practising Cell

I begin with a curious statement: maybe Cell is not principally about prayer. Prayer is an extraordinarily wide thing. When in 1992, Richard Foster penned what may have become a modern classic, simply called *Prayer*, he unpacked no less than 21 different kinds of prayer, grouped into three aspects: moving inwards seeking transformation; moving upwards seeking intimacy; and moving outwards seeking ministry. My understanding is that Cell is about transformation by God and intimacy with God, of which praying is one element. A parallel is that a loving relationship is something deeper than the conversation that animates it, the practices that express it and the time it takes.

I want to be helpful to readers who want to explore Cell. It would be arrogant and foolish to try to make this book about 'how to pray'. There are a host of other books that do that. I am going to try to unpack two approaches to transformation and intimacy – or becoming changed within – that I have found valuable.

Thoughts about our thoughts

We all know that in prayer our thoughts wander. Our thoughts also play a large part in the rest of our lives. Sometimes we are driven by them; at other times they distract us. We even know despair about them and their obstinate patterns. What is to be done? For five years now, I have found the writing of Meg Funk OSB very insightful. I can't try, in a few paragraphs, to catch all that she has distilled across five small books and her lifetime of spiritual guiding, but giving an introductory flavour of what I have found so far pays my debt to her and commends your own exploration.

In her first book, *Thoughts Matter*, she draws on the desert tradition with its emphasis on winning the battle of the thoughts that pass through our minds. The monks quickly found that going to the desert did not mean they had left troublesome thoughts behind them. So these had to be contended with. The eight thoughts cluster around three that afflict the body – food, sex and things; two which afflict the mind – anger and dejection; and three that afflict the soul – *acedia* (weariness of soul), vainglory and pride. Later these forces were called the seven deadly sins (merging the last two), but that led to an emphasis on condemnation of sin at the end of the process, whereas the heart of the training needs to fall at the start, with the thoughts. How does this training work?

First, we have to notice that we have thoughts. Even that way of putting it introduces a key concept: *we are not our thoughts*. I had never seen it like that before and had tended to blame myself for having thoughts I am not going to name here. This realisation ties in with the word 'afflict', used by Funk, and now makes liberating sense to me. Thoughts come to us, often unbidden, though also because we gave them a home last time. They might arise from a situation, from meeting another person, from a dream or from God, or they might be a diabolical temptation.

So, second, after noticing them, we must seek to discern the source. Are they good or bad, noble or base, invitations for now, later or never?

Third, we have the freedom and power to think another thought, which is to refuse the first one. To take a trivial example, 'Shall I have another coffee?' 'No, I don't need it and it would be far nicer to have it later with X.'

Sometimes, fourth, we can resolve to bring in a contrasting thought: 'Instead of sitting moping, I'll go and do the washing-up, or mow the lawn, or clean the car.' (Work is one good antidote to *acedia*.)

Treat them this way, and the initial thought will pass. It came, it went. Fail to do that, entertain the thought and what happens? The desert fathers noted a progression: thoughts that are dwelt on become desires; desires considered become passions; passions acted on by consent at that point become sins; repeated sins are vices and become habits that hook us.

Cell is where we learn the conscious practice by which thoughts are identified, confronted, refused and reshaped. I am reminded of Paul's advice, 'We take captive every thought to make it obedient to

Christ' (2 Corinthians 10:5). But maybe even 'taking them captive' invites dangerous collusion with them, and Funk urges it is better to be rid of them. Brother Lawrence agrees: 'Thoughts spoil everything. All evil begins there. We must take care to set them aside as soon as we observe them.'[24]

The practice of winning this long-term thought-battle will be tested in all seven spaces. Cell is like the training ground and practice pitch where we learn new skills, work on our weaknesses, hone good habits, memorise maxims and build attentive watching reflexes. The other six communal spaces are like the match where, in the rush and tumble of life, those skills and attitudes are tested in reality. The match may well show up what still needs more work in the training ground – like successfully taking a penalty under pressure or not getting red-carded when things go wrong!

Funk's books contain much more to say as she unpacks applying such general principles to each affliction in turn. Like a good doctor, she does not apply one medicine to all conditions. In later books, like *Tools Matter*, she introduces practices such as guarding the heart, repentance, ceaseless prayer, kinds of fasting, *lectio divina* (ways of sacred reading), manual work, use of the cell, vigils, consulting an elder and Benedict's ladder of humility. I trail these to indicate that there is much more to learn, but I am convinced that Cell is where the practices of the inner life are learnt and practised. She puts it this way: 'I discovered that the primary purpose of the Benedictine culture was to train one for the inner life.'[25] The focus on the inner life ties in with Jesus' words, 'Out of the heart come evil thoughts' (Matthew 15:19). What we truly are is what we are within. Funk calls Cell 'the place of truth'.[26] The fruit tells you what kind of tree it is and whether it is healthy.

But this emphasis on what we are urged to do, and with discipline can often do, needs to be balanced by what God alone does in and for us. In my 55 years of consciously following Christ, seeking to live by, yet straying from, that dynamic balance has been an endless story. A bookmark on my desk has the words of Augustine: 'Without God we cannot; without us God will not.'

God's delight

Once again I begin with a grateful acknowledgement, here to Mark Clavier. His book draws on the experience and theology of Augustine of Hippo to address the sharp issue of how Christians may effectively and attractively resist the clarion calls of consumerism.[27] In short, both consumerism and Christianity appeal for our allegiance. The appeal in advertising is seldom about the content of the product or the logic of buying it. No, consumerism appeals to our emotions, through selling an image, our right of choice, personal identity, peer pressure and desire. In Cicero's classic description of how argument, or rhetoric, works, persuasion is achieved less by the *logos* – the rational – and more by the *pathos* – the persuasive appeal which causes us to desire what is being argued or sold. Augustine grew up imbibing Cicero and using the skills he taught. In his long process of becoming a Christian, Augustine knew the stage of accepting its truth – the *logos* of the rhetorical case. But he found that the continuing desire for the delights of his prior life were stronger than any self-generated delight in God. In the sort of terms used by Paul in Romans 7, Augustine knew what was right but found that knowledge of the law merely condemned him. It left him powerless to desire what the *logos* in his head told him. I guess there are few readers who have not known this dilemma either at some point or for many years.

What is the way forward? How can a triumphing desire for God overcome the powerful desires and delights sold shamelessly to us by our dominant consumer culture and our own desires? Merely contrasting the worldviews of Christianity and consumerism will not help us any more than Augustine found, or Paul achieved, by knowing the law. Augustine himself discovered, and therefore taught, that God takes the initiative. God acts as the divine persuader, or rhetorician, of delight. But this is not by word alone. Delight in God is God's gift by the Holy Spirit. 'God's love has been poured out into our hearts through the Holy Spirit, who has been given to us' (Romans 5:5). This quote Augustine uses over 200 times. The link between love and delight is that all true love is a delight.

For the first time I understood that the phrase 'the love of God' has two applications and meanings. The first I knew through John 3:16 – the love *of* God; that is, God's love for us as creator and saviour. But the second meaning, and this aspect is what is at work here, is the love *for* God, whose origin is between the members of the Trinity. Indeed for Augustine, he understood the Holy Spirit as, in part, being the love between Father and Son.[28] It is this love, as a gift, which enters us by the Holy Spirit. Thus, within us, a delight in God is planted. We are caught up in the very love between the members of the Trinity. In that sense Christianity is not so much a belief, much less a set of morals; it is being encountered by Jesus Christ and receiving the Holy Spirit.

This understanding chimes in with the passionate love seen in the life of Francis. I see it in the 17th-century 'conversations' of Brother Lawrence, shot through with his being captivated by the love for God and joy in God, which were equally present in his Cell or at the kitchen sink.[29] Here Cell overflowed into his life. Or take the words of a slightly earlier French saint, Bishop François de Sales (1567–1622): 'To desire to love God is to love to desire Him, and hence to love Him, for love is the root of all desire.'[30] It resonates with the title of C.S. Lewis' spiritual biography, *Surprised by Joy*. It lies behind the language of 'Amazing grace, how sweet the sound.' It makes possible beginning to keep the great commandment, 'Love the Lord your God with all your heart and with all your soul and with all your mind and with all your strength' (Mark 12:30). It fits with the charismatic experience variously called baptism, filling or release of the Spirit. In my life it fits with my own utter abiding delight when I committed myself to Christ as a teenager. Here is the life of prayer as intimacy.

However, this precious delightful gift does not solve everything. We continue to live with both the struggles of Romans 7 and the glories of Romans 8. Similarly competing delights – from God and from the world and the evil one – will be our lot until heaven. In that struggle we will be aided considerably by two factors. One is fighting the thought-battle in the Cell, as Funk helps us grasp. The second, as Clavier urges, is by being part of a church community which seeks to embody and demonstrate the love of God which has been poured into our hearts by the Spirit; in the terms of this book, by living out the other six spaces well. Both factors address transformation.

Cell as a place of honesty and puzzle

The desirable virtue of honesty lives with the puzzle about who we really are, because Cell strips us. I am conscious of how often we are posing. 'Smile,' commands the photographer, no matter what burdens our soul is bearing. In public ministry, often we live out role not inner reality. The gulf between the inner me and the perceived image is disturbing. Be afraid when you are called an expert. Even Funk can wonder, 'Am I yet really a nun?'[31] The puzzle is encapsulated well by lines from a poem Dietrich Bonhoeffer wrote in prison, sometime between 1943 and 1945.[32]

Who am I? They often tell me
I stepped from my cell's confinement
Calmly, cheerfully, firmly,
Like a squire from his country-house…
Am I then really all that which other men tell of?
Or am I only what I myself know of myself?
Restless and longing and sick, like a bird in a cage…
Weary and empty at praying, at thinking, at making,
Faint and ready to say farewell to it all?

Who am I? They mock me these lonely questions of mine.
Whoever I am, thou knowest, O God, I am thine.

Application questions

- Where, if anywhere, do you experience Cell?

- If you have a place, what characterises it?

- How could a parent of children under five attempt Cell?

- Write down your understanding of the saying, 'Go sit in your cell, and your cell will teach you everything.'

- What have you found are the challenges to overcome to allow Cell to work?

- What benefits have you found from being in the Cell?

- How might you begin to practise Cell differently, having read this chapter?

✤ 4 ✤

CHAPEL
corporate public worship

What does Chapel mean?

Everybody agrees what a chapel is. Or do we? Very different answers would be given by an English Anglican and a Welsh Free Church member. For the former it is usually a quiet, smaller worship space within a larger ecclesial building, be that a parish church or a cathedral; for the latter it is a denominational and cultural identity and the building used for congregational worship. Yet another variant is a chapel serving a larger complex, such as a dedicated room in a school, barracks, a prison or an airport. In the monastic world it was one location among several on the site. Its being only one building in the grounds helps us to ask two questions. What is it for? And what is it *not* for, which the other places are there to do? In other words, what does Chapel do in relation to the other places?

The relationship between Chapel and Cell

Chapel and Cell contrasted

Chapel can be sharply contrasted with Cell, in relation to the worship of God and prayer to him.

Chapel	Cell
Chapel is a public space	Cell must be private space
Chapel deals in corporate worship	Cell processes private thoughts
Chapel can be rich in stimulus	Cell is intentionally bare
Chapel is led by others	Cell must be led by you
Chapel is liturgical	Cell contains extemporary prayer
Chapel teaches by the liturgical	Cell passes beyond words to intimacy with God
Chapel remains structured	Cell may well include the emotional and turbulent
Chapel stays measured	Cell will contain significant moments of spontaneity
Chapel is to exalt God	Cell allows God to deal with us
Chapel uses many flowing words	In Cell, a few words, or even silence, may pierce us

Chapel and Cell as complementary

I hope it is clear that this list of divergences does not make one of them better than the other. The point is that they do different work and that we need both. Neither can be a substitute for the other. Sometimes it is tempting to value one more highly. Anglicans and Catholics might favour Chapel, while Charismatics and Free Church members might promote the values of Cell. There can be a tension between Cell and Chapel. I urge that we hold on to both ends and maintain the tension, rather than cut the link with both parties, retreating into adversarial corners.

Holding the tension is exemplified in Francis' own life. His most profound moments of spiritual experience were in solitude. He usually sought this when spontaneity and response to promptings of the Spirit led him into spiritual and emotional responses. Therefore in liturgical worship he deliberately restrained himself 'so as not to give offence or disclose the divine intoxication'.[1] Equally, early biographers note he received Holy Communion often and so devoutly as to inspire others.[2] Francis valued both. The art is living truly with God in both places and cooperating with what they do differently. Dietrich Bonhoeffer's book *Life Together* is a witness to this partnership. He calls chapter 2 'The day with others' and chapter 3 'The day alone', writing in the latter, 'The day together will be unfruitful without the day alone, both for the fellowship and for the individual.' He presents the former as characterised by speech and the latter by silence; the one coming out of the other and both in response to the word of God. He also likens this dynamic relationship to the life of a family living closely together in which 'regular times of quiet are absolutely necessary'.[3] So Chapel and Cell is a partnership of complementary difference.

This connects with the overlap of Chapel and Cell as experienced by a growing number today. I link this to Abbot Jamison's helpfully suggesting that the word 'prayer' has two meanings. The general one is 'all activity by which people raise their hearts and minds towards God, by which they address the divine "you"'. Such prayer is about inner intention and can be prompted by a variety of circumstances: irenic, tragic or banal. There is also a second, more precise, meaning: 'a prayer is a specific form of words addressing God', by which he includes those already written and the spontaneous, 'but it is always a set of words'.[4] Meditation and contemplation are prayer of the first kind, usually used in Cell; prayers in the second sense include all the public elements of Chapel worship. Both are about keeping the awareness of God alive during the whole day, and the first kind needs the supporting structure of community prayer, as well as the presence of community life. This is why being a hermit is seen as spiritually harder and reserved only for those who have already shown they can live the communal life.

A further complication of this overlap is research showing that a large number of Christians have stopped attending congregations and only attend small groups or are solitary Christians.[5] As more Christians find themselves alienated from congregational life, the functions of Cell and Chapel are being fused within their own homes. In this walk they may be fortified by written resources such as *Celtic Daily Prayer* (CDP) or material on the internet. As individuals use these liturgies, 'Chapel' happens in their Cell as the set readings become *lectio divina*, prayer purposefully wanders and spontaneous prayer grows out of the structured. The things that are missing in this private practice are the corporate, Eucharist and singing. Singing opens the joys of harmony and cooperation and the use of varied instruments (but, please, not dominance by the organist or worship leader). Northumbria Community understanding is that we are called to live both *alone* and *together*, and this development looks like too much of the former. We may be seeing a sad growth of de-churched orphaned hermits among the growing number of non-attending Christians.

So if I daily sit in my study at home, in my favoured armchair, and pray the CDP office, including intercession for others, am I doing Cell or Chapel? Frankly I don't know. All I know is that this concise, closely structured prayer proves to be the platform from which spontaneous prayer bursts. I have learnt to value both elements. I need the structured to guard me from the cast of mind that otherwise could be unduly introspective, self-centred and self-critical. I value too those moments of unfettered delight when something beyond the structured happens.

Data from the focus groups

The groups I talked with sensed some of these issues. One group called Chapel the corporate Cell, and the Northumbria members called it 'an alone and together place'. People instinctively knew Chapel included a cluster of related phrases: corporate worship, intentional gathering, worship by the whole community and collective prayer, all of which are unifying and ways of giving back to God. The evangelists of Church Army added, 'If open to non-members, Chapel can have a witness,' and 'It is a place where commitments are made.' Those making vows within Northumbria Community at the mother house do so in its chapel, as do evangelists admitted to Church Army. Benedict concurs: 'He comes before the whole community in the oratory' (58.17).

The plural voice of central texts used in Chapel, such as '*Our* Father' and '*We* believe', emphasises the togetherness. It is prayer with, to and for others. Its contents are communal ritual, liturgy and sacraments. And liturgical prayer aims to be concise, crafted and orthodox, yet moving. It is also a discipline by which we come with others to God, whether we like it or not, acting as a reminder to love God and others.

The groups also picked up that Chapel has a function in relation to the other six. The Church Army people called it 'a focus for the rest of the functions' and noted that Chapel occurs at fixed focal points in the day, led by authorised people. Those from Northumbria said, 'It pulls together the other places.' They have a phrase for this and call the seeking of God 'the one thing necessary'.

I value these comments; they underline the importance of Chapel, both in itself and in relation to the other six spaces. Yet make chapel services the whole, and the dynamism and difference between the seven spaces is lost. If Chapel is like a motorway service station, the point is not to stay on the forecourt. It is no accident that the Church of England Communion service ends with 'Go in peace to love and serve the Lord.'

Chapel in the various Rules

In the Rules the word 'Chapel' is absent. Often this space is called the 'Oratory'. Many sections of the Rules refer to its purpose. This is called either 'the divine office' or 'the canonical hours', that is, liturgical, corporate, readings and prayers. There is no doubt the space existed and that corporate worship is seen as a contender to be the highest priority.

Immediately after Benedict's longest chapter in his Rule, on the ladder of humility, come 13 chapters dealing with public worship by the community. It is the single largest portion of the Rule of Benedict and unswerving about its priority: 'Indeed, nothing is to be preferred to the work of God' (43.3). The Celtic Rule of Ailbe says the monk 'should be faithful to the obligation of intercession' and 'be constant in prayer, never forgetting the canonical hours', which are 'regarded as primary'.[6] The Rule of Carthage concurs: 'Let us frequent the holy church for each canonical hour.'[7] Worship regulations are the longest chapter in the Rule of Columbanus, but only a minor section in Francis. Other work is set aside when signals for Chapel occur. Usually there are two separate signals (Rule of Benedict 48.12), a practice of ringing bells followed both at Nether Springs and Hilfield Friary.

Chapel's purpose, priority and singularity are made clear in the following injunction from the Rule of Benedict: 'The oratory (the place of prayer and praise) ought to be what it is called and nothing else is to be done or stored there' (52.1).[8] Such a verse should make untidy vergers beware, but it could also alarm progressives who want to see kitchens, loos and cafes in churches. This raises the question of whether our so-called 'churches' are just chapels. Await chapter 11 for the unpacking of that issue.

The word 'vigils', meaning prayer times, is also characteristic (8.3, 11.1, referring to evening and morning prayers). The word evokes patience, steadfastness and even nobility of purpose. Attention beyond external compliance is crucial, even if elusive in practice. 'Let us stand to sing the psalms in such a way that our minds are in harmony with our voices' (19.7). The content of worship laid down makes vigilance necessary; no wonder Benedictines promise stability, fidelity and obedience (58.17).

The Psalms are seen as core in this tradition, all 150 being said weekly, with particular emphasis on Psalm 119 (18.7–11),[9] not to do so being seen as 'extreme indolence' (18.23–25). For Benedict knows the desert fathers said them all in a day. The Irish Celtic practice was equally tough: the psalms take precedence over all else, with 30 said every day.[10] Benedict also wants readings from Old Testament and New Testament, many said by heart, a gospel reading and prayers.

Psalm 119, with its 176 verses and 22 acrostic sections, held a special place in Celtic spirituality. It was held that its repetition every day for a year would free a soul from hell and to recite it at the outset would bring good fortune on a journey. Known as the *Beati*, it was seen by a tenth-century mystical commentary as an allegory of the 176 paces in the spiritual journey the soul makes from Babylon to Jerusalem, or hell to heaven. So the commentator urges, 'May every wise man who hears it examine it carefully at all times.'[11]

Despite this list, Benedict requires that 'prayer should be short and pure, unless perhaps it is prolonged under the inspiration of divine grace. In community, however, prayer should always be brief' (20.4–5). Commentators concur: 'Chapel time was swift and strong, quick and deep, brief but soul-shaking.'[12] The Rule of Comgall agrees: 'Do not practise long, drawn-out devotions, rather give yourself to prayer at intervals, as you would to food. Pious humbug is an invention of the Devil.'[13]

The sevenfold pattern of offices,[14] Chittister says, fitted with the changing of the Roman imperial guard. Often Christians have taken known secular patterns and employed them, such as Salvationist William Booth or, much earlier, the Franciscan Jacapone composing words to contemporary popular melodies. The seven offices fell within a Mediterranean day that ended with unlit night shortly after 6.00 pm and so, incredibly to us, could start after eight hours' sleep at 2.00 am.[15] At the Reformation, Archbishop Thomas Cranmer reduced the daily offices to morning and evening prayer, hoping the laity might attend.

Both my 2009 sojourns were in communities that used four offices: morning, midday, late-afternoon and night prayer. The modern

Franciscan manual *The Principles* sees Eucharist as central, daily being the ideal. It sits within four daily offices, which prepare for and end the day and offer structured meditation. Attention is drawn, day 16, to inner attitudes so that attendance at them is not in a 'formal or careless spirit' but rather 'a devotion from the heart'.

These times of structured prayer create the rhythms of the day. Or, to use another image, the times of Chapel provide the punctuation that makes sense of the paragraph of a day. For me, injecting the short Northumbria Community midday office, followed by a period of quiet until lunchtime, remains the most countercultural to today's 24/7 culture and the workaholic life I am tempted to lead. Now in retirement I have begun to resurrect this midday practice to give more shape to a more unpredictable life of many smaller pieces. As this book goes to press, I have been in lockdown isolation, and the practice has been a gift shaping these uncertain, self-determined days. I have found its canticle and blessing astonishingly apposite: 'Teach us, dear Lord, to number our days that we may apply our hearts unto wisdom,' and, 'Let nothing disturb thee, nothing affright thee, all things are passing, God never changeth.'[16]

Liturgical highs and lows

Psalms as a delight and a problem

I have always found the heavy use of the Psalms presents a dilemma. In my 2009 sabbatical I recited large numbers of them. Often the printed text was marked with a lozenge or asterisk halfway through a verse, placed at the end of its first line. It indicates a short break in recitation. This is a device invented by, and beloved of, some Franciscan liturgists. The theory behind it is that this is a way of paying attention to Hebrew parallelism, a poetic device by which successive lines (usually two) say much the same thing, but they might do so in subtly different ways or even contrasting ones. An example of the former is: 'The heavens declare the glory of God; the skies proclaim the work of his hands' (Psalm 19:1). So the lozenge points up the parallelism.

I was entertained recently at a Sheffield diocesan clergy study day. This rationale was given to the gathering and then put into practice in the closing worship. Immediately there was confusion. There was no agreed view of how long the short break should be. Different parts of the congregation came in at different times. No one could give any meaningful attention to a single parallelism, because they were all struggling to know when to open their mouths.

This practice I regard, first, as grammatically bizarre. What sense does it make to have a lozenge-induced pause at a comma or semicolon but to bat on without a break through a full stop at the end of the verse? I wonder what Lynne Truss, the 'apostle of the apostrophe' and entertaining and passionate writer about good grammar, would say of it.[17] Second, it is educationally confusing. The emphasis is on the avoidance of saying the psalm wrongly rather than a pondering of what the text means. Third, it is psychologically difficult. The uninitiated are reduced to mumbling, uncertain when the post-lozenge line starts up again. While those familiar with it cope with this oddity of flow, I suspect they have no time whatsoever to ponder the meaning of an incessant torrent of parallelisms. It is a classic Anglican example of a plausible theory being completely impractical and even spiritually unhelpful. If we must have a pause, let's do it at the end of a verse, not halfway through.

So overall, the public recitation of the Psalms has been a mixed liturgical experience, and my rant is over. I do see the value of walking through the varied landscape of the Psalms, delighting in their high moments, suffering alongside their black days and even being appalled at their occasional arrogance, revenge and rage. Yet the liturgy forces me to travel through them quicker than the stereotype of the worst American tourist. Yet at the same time I agree with Chittister, who reflects on this biblical content in liturgy: 'A full prayer life must be based on a total immersion in all the life experiences to which the psalms are a response.'[18] I do not want to escape them, but I need time and space to inhabit them. I acknowledge that without the Psalms our worship is shorn of evident delight in God and his creation. Without them we avoid admission of lament, protest and complaint, which are also part of the complex spiritual life of normal Christian people. The prayer of lament (godly sorrow, not cross criticism) needs to be given space in our worship. Lament might be for the failures of the Church, our being in a new kind of exile or injustice in the world. We need help to manage this overall diet better.

Words, words, words

A number of my friends complain that many recent liturgies are very wordy. Archbishop George Carey wrote the foreword to *Celebrating Common Prayer* and pursued Archbishop Cranmer's hope of lay people finding daily patterns to prayer, instead of personal prayer being 'unstructured and haphazard'.[19] On the one hand it contains jewels of prayers. I think here of the longer post-Communion prayer: 'Father of all, we give you thanks and praise, that when we were still far off you met us in your Son and brought us home. Dying and living he declared your love.' The newly included wider set of canticles I value. On the other hand, I find it a very complex book, well beyond the so-called 'average layperson'. Its contents and choices are more complicated than memory can serve, and its services are simply too long, not least the baptism service. Most of the recent eucharistic liturgies and their great thanksgivings also suffer from the same bursting of water from a liturgical dam wall.

I am grateful to Mark Earey for writing *Beyond Common Worship*.[20] He writes from inside the Liturgical Commission, yet he knows that in tailoring liturgy to varied contexts, not least among non-book cultures and among the non-churched, we need to move from central precise control to trust, based on local leaders having liturgical values and instincts, not slavishly following nationally approved texts. Bishop Colin Buchanan, who taught me liturgy, used to quip that we have moved from serving up 'meals on wheels' –

cooked centrally and distributed locally – to teaching people how to cook. Related to this is the fact that for the past few decades we have been living through unpredictable transitions towards a key concept. By this process the understanding of the essence of liturgy has changed. From the 16th century until the 1980s liturgy used to be understood as having an agreed, enforceable set text, from which deviation was forbidden. From the publication of *Patterns for Worship* in 1989, we began to think that liturgical worship was more about shapes that are then furnished with appropriate words.[21] But since around 2006, some have been arguing that liturgy is about identifiable shared values, which then lead to appropriate shapes and contextually crafted texts.[22] I have seen this operating in the worship created thoughtfully in fresh expressions of church.

Another wish is that we find modern equivalents of Cranmer to write concise poetic prose that is mentally portable. The English language, peppered with phrases from the 1662 Book of Common Prayer, shows that it's possible. William Tyndale did much the same in the 1530s in his translation of the Bible. His crisp yet memorable phrasing makes up the bulk of the better-known Authorised Version of 1611. Benedict knew this need for portability, and chapter 50 of the Rule expects Chapel to occur when monks are dispersed on journeys; those working far away will say the offices 'where they are'; they 'observe them as best they can' (50.3–4).

The gift of liturgy

An extreme yet instructive example of praying the offices 'as best you can' connects with one of the values of liturgical prayer. Terry Waite was an envoy of the Archbishop of Canterbury and captured in 1987 in Beirut while trying to negotiate for the release of hostages. He was held captive in demanding conditions for four years till 1991. In his 1993 book *Taken on Trust*, he explained that he was able to remember and pray the poetic words of the 1662 Book of Common Prayer more easily than texts of scripture. The principle is that we are formed by what we regularly pray. In much easier circumstances I find something similar with the words of the offices of the Northumbria Community prayer book. It was easy to learn them all by heart. Thus when on a train or woken in the middle of the night, I have access to the sort of spiritual words my busy or fevered brain can take refuge in. I am stilled and recentred. I know and have met the suspicion of some Free Church people that such praying is but 'vain repetition' or the 'babbling pagan prayer in many words' dismissed by Jesus (Matthew 6:7). Rather, these familiar words have also become part of the furniture of the house of my Christian discipleship.

I suggest liturgical prayer works like a door. It is possible to admire it or dislike it when viewed from the outside, but both responses to its architectural value mean we have not responded to what it is for. It is to be passed through. Similarly, liturgical texts can be either praised for their poetry or thought boring by their length, but neither of those responses is the point. Precisely because of its familiarity, made more accessible by its striking phrasing, we mentally pass through the words to the meaning and the person of God behind the meaning. Do that, and truly praying the liturgy means entering a related spiritual world beyond its door.

Moreover, the fact that its times are planned and its gathering is intentional provides a structure; it is a discipline by which we come with others to God, whether we like it or not. We also meet others, whether we like them or not. Benedict insists that the entire Lord's Prayer is recited morning and evening. Why? It is said 'for all to hear, because thorns of contention are likely to spring up' (13.12). What a realist Benedict is about conflict in community. To be honest about the need to pray 'forgive us our sins *as we forgive* those who sin against us' is a necessary part of the life of any community.

Perhaps the Benedictine attitude to Chapel is summarised either in his words, 'The divine presence is everywhere... We should believe this to be especially true when we celebrate the divine office' (19.1–2), or in the words of a present-day abbess, 'Benedictine spirituality says... we must regularly seek to find God in one time and space that enables us to recognise God more easily in every other one.'[23] I find this balance helpful. Chapel is essential, but it is not everything, and everything should not be collapsed into it. This has significant implications for how and when we use the much bigger word 'church' and what we expect its buildings to be able to do. Are most of our 'churches' actually only chapels?

The value to put on Chapel

So how much should we invest in Chapel, and what attitudes might we bear in mind? A Franciscan comment is salutary in a world of need and injustice. The first Franciscan mission to England in 1224 immediately built a simple chapel in a single day at Canterbury.[24] Today Hilfield chapel embodies virtues of simplicity and yet transcendence. *The Principles*, day 6, refers to 'the house of God, which it is right and seemly with proper moderation to adorn'. Chapels need to be evocative, but they don't need to be grand if they are working with the other six spaces. Moreover, corporate worship has integrity and is nurtured only if there is health in the other six spaces. The prophet Amos had strong words about the delusion of apparent devotion in worship when accompanied by unethical lives.

Throughout exploration of the seven spaces, I realise that they only become sacred if the way we inhabit them is spiritually healthy. Let's apply that to Chapel. External liturgical perfection counts for little in itself. This links to Jesus' saying that the Father seeks those worshipping him 'in the Spirit and in truth' (John 4:23). It connects too with the New Testament emphasis that the temple is no longer a building but is both Christ and Christians (1 Corinthians 3:16–17; Ephesians 2:21–22; 1 Peter 2:4–5). How we are in ourselves, not just where we are in the seven spaces, is what counts. In the same spirit, Benedict counsels those on the ladder of humility (chapters 5–7), 'Ascending all those steps of humility, the monk will quickly arrive at that "perfect love of God which casts out fear"… He will now begin to observe without effort, as though naturally from habit… out of love for Christ, good habit and delight in virtue' (67–70). If the heart is right, so much else comes right.

Application questions

- If life in Cell is being spiritually productive, for what reasons do Christians need Chapel?
- Why would you say, honestly, you go to your church's worship service?
- What do you find you gain from its public worship?
- Are you frustrated by it? If so, in what way?
- What part do you think public worship should play in a Christian community?
- What elements of being a Christian community cannot be provided by Chapel?

✢ 5 ✢

CHAPTER
making decisions

My wake-up call about Chapter

Early in my exploration of the seven sacred spaces, I was blind to Chapter being its own place. That's ironic in view of its decision-making function and my controlling behaviour. Is it a parable of the need to have effective Chapters to avoid the danger of unaccountable, self-appointed thinkers and leaders? Eventually I heard the message.

There is therefore no feedback from the Church Army focus groups to report on the role of Chapter, but the Northumbria Community group set me right, insisting on this space and tracing some of its contours. They taught me that Chapter is mostly about *how* decisions are made in community, because the health of a Christian community is affected every bit as much by the manner in which decisions are taken as by the content of those decisions. They prized Chapter, because of the consensual, relational, communal style of Northumbria Community. By contrast, pushing through 'the right thing' by a wrong process, manner or style is more damaging than helpful. What will future historians make of the Brexit saga?

Their phrases for what occurs in Chapter were 'communication, corporate discussion, debate and disagreement, intentional accountability'. All of those words are easy to say and less easy to do well. The accountability they understood was both of the leaders to the wider community and of elected members to those who put them there. As such, the essence of Chapter is a social and governmental function more than a specific building, although in the monastic communities I have lived among, they usually occur in a known, public, recreational space. In all these cases the shape supports the consensual style.

In that it is about making decisions, it is no accident that in specific Chapter houses, such as the Cistercian one reconstructed in Cîteaux, France,[1] there is a large lectern, from which either a chapter of the Rule or a chapter of the Bible is read.[2] In both cases those called to be decision-makers themselves sit under a higher authority. The decision-making itself needs to be in the right spirit, which the texts of both scripture and the order's Rule commend.

Qualities that aid Chapter

As soon as decisions have to be made, issues of power raise their head. Such meetings can easily be places of tension or competition, where issues dominate over relationships and, worse, procedural manoeuvring triumphs over common sense. As soon as someone says, 'Point of order, Mr Chairman', part of me groans. Yet all groups have to make decisions, because they have a common life and because life presents us with choices. So how do we do it better?

Scripture contains plenty of examples of good and bad decisions. Eve and Adam didn't do so well, nor did Solomon's arrogant and headstrong son Rehoboam (1 Kings 12). Solomon's track record was mixed, and Moses had to learn to listen and take Jethro's advice (Exodus 18). The Jewish council's meetings struggled to make good decisions, despite the commendable wisdom of Gamaliel (Acts 4—6). The early church didn't find it easy balancing tradition and innovation, but found a way forward (Acts 15).

Chapter 79

Mutual respect

Yet despite Chapter being under a common authority, the Northumbria Community group were realists who knew that Chapter is a place of tension. Tension can be good or bad. It can speak of the challenge of a worthwhile balance being held, such as dealing with both the practical and the spiritual or holding on to unity while living with diversity. Or tension can refer to the atmosphere when there are disagreeable currents running round the room, when stomachs churn, accusations fly, words wound and tempers rise. If the positive sense is to be followed and the bad one combatted, then the group affirmed 'mutual respect' as being one key quality to pursue.

Humility

I suspect that mutual respect is the consequence of a core quality, prized equally by Benedictines and Franciscans – humility. In the Rule of Benedict, chapter 7 on humility is easily the longest, running to seven pages. In *Finding Sanctuary* Abbot Jamison devotes a whole worthwhile chapter to it, calling it one of the three key qualities: 'In his Rule, Benedict places humility at the heart of his insights about monastic life.'[3] Jamison in his commentary sets humility in the context of our awe of God and seeking his will. Growing in humility (or ascending its ladder) will take patience, self-honesty (not the creeping false humility of Uriah Heep), living by the values of the Rule, speaking gently and modestly, and integrity between inner and outer humility. Humility helps all seven spaces become sacred. It connects to a third attitude specifically related to the function of Chapter.

Renouncing judgement

Chapter was not just the place of decisions but also of determining and applying discipline. In the desert tradition there are stories of Chapter being used to judge and, if necessary, condemn failing brothers. But it often didn't work out like that. Several cases are cited in Rowan Williams' book *Silence and Honey Cakes*. The most visual and thus memorable is of such a meeting to which Abba Moses was invited, chose to be absent and was then fetched. He arrived carrying a leaky jug of water. Of course it was noticed and the story continues:

> The others came out to meet him and said, 'What is this, Father?' The old man said to them, 'My sins run out behind me and I cannot see them, yet here I am coming to sit in judgement on the mistakes of someone else.' When they heard this, they called off the meeting.[4]

The story embodies what Williams explains: spiritual life is not detached mysticism; it necessitates 'living in concrete community'. The connection is profound, quoting Anthony: 'Our life and our death is with our neighbour. If we win our brother we win God. If we cause our brother to stumble we have sinned against Christ.'[5] Indeed the Desert Fathers call such a spirit of judgement 'death to the neighbour'.

Other stories of the Desert Fathers show the wise helping the failing through prior admission of their own continued vulnerability and weakness, not harsh condemnation of sinfulness. This in turn prompts both the person who is the discouraged failure to be merciful to himself and the self-satisfied pretender to honesty. Williams sees 'the goal as reconciliation with God by way of this combination of truth and mercy'.[6] It is truth, not tolerance, to face up to sin. It is mercy, not harshness, to offer humble self-knowledge, disclosed among the wise. The result 'is to renounce the power of judgement over someone else' and one of the 'essentials of the monastic life'.[7] It recalls Jesus' challenge to 'let any one of you who is without sin be the first to throw a stone' (John 8:7) and his jibe about removing a plank from our own eyes (Luke 6:42). Quite often renouncing judgement comes up in the epistles (Romans 2:1–4; 14:13; Galatians 6:1–2; James 4:11–12).

Chapter 81

This desirable rejection of judgemental attitudes is not an ancient expression of today's view, which puts unquestionable value on 'tolerance' and the autonomous individual. These in turn lead to a deeper problem in which 'anything goes' and there is no objectivity, no agreed values, and the ways to find them are beyond our reach. We have confusion of standards; community breakdown and social anarchy are not so far away.

David, a long-standing friend and vicar experienced the latter. He was exploring Chapter with members of his parish and asked two linked questions: 'How do we do accountability, as disciples walking together as a community with Jesus?' and 'Who knows about the battles you have to deal with in your Cell?' He met fierce resistance rooted in inviolable privacy and the rejection of accountability. All historic understandings of Chapter would find those reactions both strange and dangerous. As he put it, reflecting on the experience:

> Accountability in decision-making helps one begin to find what might be right, good and true. My logic is simply that I am not the truth; Jesus is the truth. We are the body of Christ and therefore fellowship and accountability within the body should help me find the truth.[8]

The danger of grumbling

Both at and after the meeting there can be an attitude to resist. Avoid grumbling or complaining. This can occur when decisions have been made that we don't approve of or were not consulted about. In the Rule of Benedict, tackling grumbling comes up often (4.39; 5.14–19; 23.1; 34.6–7; 35.19; 40.8–9; 41.5; 53.18). It ranges over decisions about food, clothing and having to serve and to obey wholeheartedly. Benedict says, 'Above all, we admonish them to refrain from grumbling' (40.9).

Acquiescence?

I recognise that these positive and peaceable attitudes may at times need to be complemented by well-argued protest and proper anger against evil, injustice, bullying or exploitation. Jesus' tough words against his critics and his action against misuse of the temple are a foundation for such legitimate opposition. Pray God we don't then become self-righteous.

Chapter in the Rules

Benedictine decisions and leadership

The Rule of Benedict, chapter 3, in an age used to imperial and imperious autocracy, lays out a remarkably consensual process: 'As often as anything important is to be done' (3.1), the abbot calls the whole community, explains the issue, hears the advice and ponders. Part of the reason (which will resonate today) that he calls 'for counsel is that the Lord often reveals what is better to the younger'. All are to 'express their opinions with all humility, and not to presume to defend their own views obstinately'. The abbot then decides what is prudent in the light of the Rule, with 'foresight and fairness' (3.3–6). For less important matters he consults with the seniors only. What a model this is in terms of attitudes and process, both for local and wider church councils. No wonder mutual respect, lack of being judgemental or grumbling, the presence of humility and discernment are needed.

Note that this chapter follows a long one on the high calling and high qualities of an abbot. The whole community elects the abbot (64.1) by the criteria of 'goodness of life and wisdom in teaching' (64.13). He distrusts his own frailty (64.15), notices the plank in his own eye (2.15) and amends his own faults (2.40). His aspiration is 'to be loved rather than feared'. However, sometimes he is taskmaster and sometimes a father (2.24).

Chapter 83

The abbot is responsible for the community's spiritual health. He acts as a physician (27.2 and 28.2–6), prescribing the ointment of encouragement and the medicine of scripture, adding his and others' prayers. But if all else fails he has to take the knife and amputate, meaning asking people to leave. Another image is of him as shepherd, giving a good example by word and action, but sometimes acting swiftly so as not to lose sheep (27.5–9 and 2.7–10). He works for loving discipline, applied with regard to varying circumstances and diverse people (2.22–32 and outworked in chapters 23–30).

Celtic and Franciscan echoes

The Celtic comment, with its own secular experience of obedience to local kings and chiefs, is brief but congruent. Monks are to listen to 'the rule of the gospel and the gentle rule of monks'. Interestingly this Rule adds later: 'the rule should not be too strict, nor too lax'.[9] This entails a corporate meeting that we could call a Chapter. Here let the abbot 'distribute tasks with justice in such a way that none of the monks be overburdened'.[10]

That balanced rule, neither strict nor lax, works out in what the leader is like too: 'The abbot should be chaste and devout, gentle yet firm. He should make known their faults to his brothers,'[11] but he also gives words of approval, especially to those who need it.[12] The Rule of Carthage urges that the abbot models the good, loves others as himself, yet roots out evil. His preaching is diligent, his learning is visible and his 'business is to heal all monks whether they be strong or weak'.[13]

The Franciscan voice reflects a similar balancing of forces and a quality of relationships lying behind it. Even by 1216 there is evidence it was known that the brothers gathered in 'the warm fellowship of their annual chapters'.[14] Section 8 of the 1223 Rule covers the General Chapter at Pentecost, held every three years, and a local annual one. *The Principles of the First Order*, day 11, says friars 'obey the decisions of the Chapter by which the common mind of the community is expressed and interpreted'. Their 1931/32 Rule lays down a weekly Tuesday morning meeting. However, no brother is required to act against his conscience. The Hilfield community gathers daily at 8.45 am for the tasks of the day, and the brothers' Chapter meets fortnightly. Each Franciscan house is its own Chapter within the order, with catholicity (connection across local expressions of church) expressed through the Provincial Chapter.[15]

I find it significant that chapter houses, as can be seen in many cathedrals, are often round or octagonal. They are designed architecturally for equal opportunity to listen and speak and for finding consensus – without corners to hide in or fire bullets from. What an attractive invitation to make our decision-making meetings better. I have learnt too that as its own space, it of course always has a doorway, but often that doorway was constructed without having a door. The message is that nothing happening there could be a secret. How different that is from the intrigue and secrecy surrounding some committee meetings.

Some practical help

I commend Colin Patterson's Grove booklet about how to learn through conflict.[16] Knowing that unhelpful conflict exists widely in the church, he faced his own need to learn how to handle this among people, not just ideas. He draws on the high view of church in Ephesians and of peace-making in James, and asks whether church people actually use the grievance procedure of Matthew 18:15–17. He explains how different people respond to conflict, and how leaders can be part of the problem when they think they are the solution. He unpacks skills like active listening, early constructive confronting, stating one's purpose and knowing when to call in outside help, as well as the slowly acquired value of consensus. He adds five ways to get groups to listen to one another better. It ends with further resources people can consult.

Chapter 85

We have no choice but to do Chapter. Life is communal and both throw up choices. But we can learn from the wisdom of the ages and current skills. The church should be a community where decision-making together becomes sacred, because it faces down grumbling and judging, and where it listens well, because it expresses mutual respect and humility. Bring it on.

Application questions

- What makes the meetings called to decide things inspiring and transformative?
- Is conflict always to be avoided? How can it be used constructively?
- What helps meetings progress beyond their difficult points?
- What might be better than decisions by majority voting?
- What is consensus and how is it discerned?

✣ 6 ✣

CLOISTER

planned and surprising meetings

Rescuing the Cloister

Suppose you heard the sentence, 'She lived a cloistered life.' For many that means she was withdrawn from life, rather otherworldly; she didn't do normal life or do people that well. She missed out on the best life can offer by excessive self-denial. To be 'cloistered' sounds shut away and sad. The word carries negative baggage. I am not using it here in this sense of withdrawal from life.

That sense of 'cloister' is a long way from what I learnt about what a cloister does. I have become fascinated by this architectural feature and what happened in its space. To start with, it is not a withdrawing place but a joining one. It was the sheltered walkway between the other spaces on the monastic site. It connected rather than separated. And in hot climates, or wet and cold ones, it protected, offering shelter as one walked between the other places.

Joining is a function that deserves noticing. To be disjointed is a significant handicap. Joining places can be underestimated until they give trouble. They are like the ligaments in the body. Footballers and skiers don't want to rupture their anterior cruciate ligament, which sits behind the kneecap and is crucial to the knee joint. If that snaps, the patient is looking at spending the rest of the season waiting for it to regrow and then to get fully fit. Joining places matter.

Cloister was where people met informally and sometimes by choice. Here was where friendships were nurtured and conversely where enemies could be made. A parallel would be the school playground. It is not part of the curriculum, but crucial in school social life.

Cloister: a word with many meanings

The various Rules I have consulted don't mention 'Cloister' by name, although all the layouts of the monastic sites I have known have joining ways between the other six spaces. Some have the classic formal four-sided covered walkways as found beside many cathedrals. This chapter is more speculative about its meaning, for I noticed the wide variety of functions assigned to Cloister by the focus groups which I consulted.

The Church Army groups mentioned that Cloister is where people could walk and talk, aiding conversations within the community. It could work as an exercise yard and recreational space. Conversely some thought it would be possible to be alone, escape, meditate, relax and watch, strolling round an empty cloister. They concurred that it was a thoroughfare, a place of connection but also potential distraction, as well as giving access to the other venues. They said that it was a place of unplanned encounters and non-planned meetings, including with those we naturally avoid.

The Northumbria Community group picked up that Cloister was a joining place, like the corridors in a house. It is about meeting people, but of course you don't know who might be just around the corner. It also valuably functioned as a place to change gear between the tones of the other different places, such as between the buzz of Refectory and the stillness of Chapel. It offered a brief walk to prepare to worship, time for a quick private prayer before a potentially difficult Chapter meeting or a moment to wash between Garden and Refectory.

Cloisters also enabled people to walk alone in prayer, to experience the rhythm of prayer on the move. It seems to be a versatile place. It affords both relaxation between the other intentional places, offering a chance of brief solitude from, but also opportunity for meeting in, community. The group mentioned it as a site for one-to-one conversations, walks in pairs, unstructured reflection and pleasant distraction, where soul friends can meet. They too saw it as the place of chance and surprising meetings. They also noted that it, along with Garden, is one of two outside places with fresh air. The hothouse of community needs such spaces.

My own guess is that Cloister has a special role as the important contact point between people who don't get on. I can imagine the thought: 'Look who's coming down the cloister now. What shall I say or do?' This is a sharp edge of the abrasion which all communities cause. My times spent in local churches and intentional communities made me coin the aphorism, 'Community is the cheese grater of the soul.' By that I mean that living in community, thus being forced to live closely with others, quickly scrapes off the mould of buried dislikes, or the rind of protective politeness, and exposes relationships for what they truly are and are not. Cloister, by its traffic in unpredictable meetings and unlikely people, speeds up that process. That is actually a good thing. Too often our communities never get real because they insist on remaining merely nice and keeping our distance.

Exploring the value called 'together'

A core phrase within Northumbria Community is 'alone and together'. That is shorthand for the ability to inhabit both states. Inability to do one of them will also damage ability to do the other. This view is rooted in Dietrich Bonhoeffer's pithy saying, 'Let him who cannot be alone beware of community. Let him who is not in community beware of being alone.'[1] In chapter 3 on Cell, I unpacked material on the necessity of being able to be alone. Now it's time to explore the importance of being together. It applies to all the other six places. I add it here because the ability to be together well may be tested most sharply in Cloister.

Sitting in your garden in the peace of the evening or being in the garden shed by yourself accompanied by a candle might be a twee expression of being alone, but it would hardly be the whole of any kind of monastic life. Because our deepest identity is being persons, being alone must be balanced by being together.[2] It is good theology to think that our view of humanity is derived from the Trinity. Tom Smail addresses just this is his book *Like Father Like Son*.[3] This starting point connects with our understanding of ourselves as being in God's image. Rowan Williams notes that our society is at the same time deeply individualistic and yet also conformist, shown for example in peer-group fashion.[4] Both forces are equally destructive of true community because neither is founded on an understanding of persons. Individuality will degenerate inexorably into competition, perhaps held back artificially by laws and rules. Free market capitalism is one example.

By contrast conformity uses rules to produce uniformity. Communism has shown us the ugly face of such societies.[5] Only community based in persons will liberate distinctive vocations yet hold them in mutual respect. Persons know the primacy of love, for it is loving relationship which comes from the other that has made me what I uniquely am. It is no surprise that marriage is described by some as the smallest example of true community, both for the centrality of love and the presence of deep difference between the couple. Love in community will always have to work with the genuine difficulty of difference, out of the knowledge of our own frailty. Cloister is the classic space where you meet difference.

Francis rejoiced in his own failure, weakness and worthlessness as the essential prompt to humility, which is the only antidote to pride, which unchecked leads to judgemental attitudes in the community.[6] The stories of the Desert Fathers frequently illustrate this desire to 'renounce the power of judgement over someone else'.[7] I teased this out more when I talked about attitudes helpful to making Chapter work well. Another brief story is as follows: 'A brother who had sinned was turned out of the church by the priest. Abba Bessarion got up and followed him; he said, "I too am a sinner."'[8] Throughout our living the value of being together well, vulnerability is writ large.

I have seen this humble self-knowledge, leading to refusal to judge and to interfere in the lives of others, come out in the common life of Northumbria Community. The community has seemed to me deliberately understated and not intense. Visitors are not buttonholed about their spiritual identity or health. The conversations among the team are always rich in jokes and leg-pulling. There is so much laughter that you suspect something serious is happening. Persons are understood and valued, held within the stability of the pattern of the prayer times, the quiet hour before lunch and shared meals. 'Together' is being lived well. These patterns create a firm structure, but at the same time they leave a style that feels loose and permission-giving. This feel is not explicitly stated but simply lived.

A pleasing subtle statement of this pair of key values, *alone* and *together*, is built into the architecture of its mother house. The house and chapel speak of the value *together*, while the grounds and the *poustinias* (tiny buildings for private prayer) testify to the necessity of *alone*. Cloister joins them all and engenders the surprising meetings. This reality is worth pointing out, so visitors can more consciously use the space to live the values. So *alone* and *together* steer the course between the rock of individualism, on which the ship of community would crash, and the whirlpool of unhealthy dependence on community into which it could be sucked.

Cloister and the Rules

I mentioned earlier that there are no direct references to Cloister in the Rules I examined, but there is a great deal said about the virtues, dangers and attitudes necessary if Cloister is to be inhabited well. Naturally these virtues apply to all the communal spaces, but I raise them here.

Benedict assumes that the brothers will meet each other and speak, as in chapter 63 on community, rank and greetings. Cloister was a significant social space. In warmer climates, its west side acted as the school room for the novices, the east side housed those handling the administration of the monastery, the south side was for storage and washing, and on the north side, into which the sunshine came, the inhabitants could sit on seats built into the wall to study.

He has much to say on attitudes to one another in community life and thus how we speak: 'A monk speaks gently… seriously and with becoming modesty, briefly and reasonably' (7.60); 'Never give a hollow greeting of peace or turn away when someone needs your love' (4.25); 'Do not repay one bad turn with another' (4.29). Joan Chittister, in her commentary on the Rule, summarises: 'Benedict says over and over, listen, learn, be open to the other. That is the ground of humility.'[9]

Abbot Jamison argues that chapters 68–72 were added in later editions of the Rule. They are all about community, perhaps written in the light of existing difficulties.[10] The lack of humility and the tendency to grumbling (see chapter 6) are frequently warned against. One community leader I met in my sabbatical described grumbling as 'the cancer of community'. Positively, monks are encouraged into mutual respect, 'supporting with the greatest patience one another's weaknesses of body or behaviour' (72.5). This fits well with my guess about Cloister. You don't know who you will meet next, and it might well be the person you despise or would rather avoid. Early on in the Rule, Benedict counsels, 'Make peace… before the sun goes down' (4.73), recognising that disputes do occur.

The input from the Celtic Rules is relational and applies to many places, but includes Cloister. Ailbe includes the following: monks are not to be vindictive, arrogant or pompous, neither to bear grudges, speak evil of others or embarrass them, nor be boastful – 'his manner should be full of affection... humble, patient and mild'.[11] Comgall offers that 'three counsels should be your guide... namely forbearance, humility and the love of God in our heart'.[12] Carthage includes no dissent, no hatred, but perseverance that is good; do not insult anyone, be not jealous or proud, show humility and joy towards friend and stranger alike.[13] Columbanus has no time for disobedient grumbling, 'garrulous verbosity', vanity or 'proud independence'. All lived 'in the company of many so that he may learn humility from one and patience from another'.[14]

The Franciscan Rule comment is slight. Section 3 of the 1223 Rule has only that friars 'should not quarrel, argue or judge others, but they should be meek, peaceful, modest, gentle and humble, speaking becomingly to all'. The longer unapproved 1221 Rule, section 11, urges the friars to love another and forbids speaking ill of each other. No direct comment is made in *The Principles of the First Order*. It is a truism that for the Franciscan their cloister is the world,[15] but this is using the term 'cloister' in yet another sense, meaning the whole monastic environment, not one architectural feature of it. Hilfield Friary does have cloisters, both round the central quad where the mid-morning break from work is held and in the many connecting places between the various buildings. It might be that the quad, too, is the initial meeting place with those seeking faith or spiritual direction, as commended in day 22 of *The Principles*.

Other snippets

Biblical material

In scripture there are plenty of meetings that happen by surprise. A good number are those in which God is the surprising arrival. Old Testament classic examples include the visit of the three strangers to Abraham and the vocational callings of Moses, Gideon and Isaiah. In the New Testament, that pattern continues in the visitation to Mary, Jesus walking with the two on the road to Emmaus, Saul outside Damascus and the Hebrews text about entertaining angelic strangers unawares.

In the three years of Jesus' public ministry, there are the more structured encounters, such as with the twelve disciples and especially with the three, but most of the healings, deliverances and even callings, such as to Zacchaeus, read as spontaneous. In that sense they are surprise meetings. From Acts and the epistles, it looks as though the early Mediterranean churches met by design – the writer to the Hebrews can entreat them not to give up meeting together (Hebrews 10:25).

Monastic diseases

I was intrigued to find in *Celtic Daily Prayer* that the Colman daily readings for January are grouped under the title of monastic diseases. They are apt when considering Cloister, but also apply to the six communal spaces as a whole.[16]

In particular, 2 January highlights three stages in entering any community: initial joy, followed by disappointment, and only then by reality. This pattern of idealism, pessimism and realism also operates in any sustained cross-cultural experience. Other days point out the dangers of stereotyping those who rub us up the wrong way and of projecting undue hope on those we are drawn to. We can be equally tempted by over-dependence on others or over-helpfulness towards others. Another trap is territorialism, believing that certain functions or places are specially mine or mine alone. Cloister is always shared, never owned. Unsurprisingly, murmuring or grumbling is cited. In view of all this, I was encouraged by the content of both day 10 and 31. The monastic life and all true holiness are characterised by falling down and getting up again – perhaps a thousand times. No wonder Jesus urged forgiveness of others by seventy times seven.

The challenge of Cloister

Cloister has a socially challenging function. I suggest it speeds up the formation of honest community. Love, humility, generosity of spirit, good listening and mutual learning, reconciliation across genuine differences – wow, that would be a church community I'd be privileged to join! Cloister puts right in your face the need to grow in all those virtues and to fight the particular temptations to grumbling, bad-mouthing, sheer hatred, judgementalism and pride that can occur when we are with others.

Application questions

- Recall a surprise positive encounter. How did it arrive and what happened?

- How could your beliefs affect those encounters which happen by chance?

- What makes meetings good?

- How might your faith, and its view of others, affect meeting people you find difficult?

- Who might find it difficult to meet you, and why?

- Where are the joining places in your church?

- What have you learnt about yourself and your walk as a Christian through surprising encounters?

✠ 7 ✠

GARDEN
the place of work

Adjusting our assumptions

I have found that people encountering this space have some unlearning to do, perhaps because most of us are modern, urban people. Here are the mental adjustments needed. For Garden, please don't mainly think of lawns and flowers; begin to think vegetables. Set aside Garden as being about idyllic rest and sylvan beauty; see it as the place of fruitful labour. Then go beyond both. The change is still more radical.

Garden needs putting back in historical context, because most people today are separated from the means of primary production. Honourable exceptions include the allotment and bread-making.[1] In days when terms like 'garden peas' and 'farmhouse bread' are an advertiser's ploy, rather than an honest description, our gardens have become hobbies, therapeutic aids and recreational spaces.[2] This is a marked change from their historic primary purpose. Historically, the garden wasn't a hobby; it was work, life and death. It was absolutely essential. The garden literally fed the refectory, or the monks starved.

What the monastic tradition calls Garden, we would call the world of work. A Christian view, going back to Genesis 1, is that work is tending the world that God has created. The ten commandments add, 'Six days you shall labour and do all your work' (Exodus 20:9). Psalm 104:22–23 teaches that when the sun rises, people go out to their work till the evening. It is the normal thing people do. Work is intrinsic to life. God has made us in his image, and we need work; without it we become dull and cease to be creative. In the New Testament, Jesus describes his life and ministry as doing his Father's work: 'I must be about my Father's business' (Luke 2:49, KJV); 'My food… [is] to finish his work' (John 4:34). Elements of that work are spelt out in John 5:19–27.

What is *opus Dei*?

With Garden we meet one of three locations that form part of the monastic understanding of 'the work of God', *opus Dei* (the other two being Chapel and Scriptorium). A foundational text is from the Rule of Benedict: 'Idleness is the enemy of the soul. Therefore, the brothers should have specified periods for manual labour, as well as for prayerful reading' (48.1). Chapter 48 of Benedict's Rule deals with both manual labour and spiritual reading, as well as how all three spaces fit around the changing seasons and the times of chapel services. It is also significant that the 1223 Franciscan Rule, chapter 5, uses the same phrasing about idleness and argues that work helps prevent the extinguishing of 'the Spirit of holy prayer and devotion'.

However, there is a spectrum, even a clash, of views about what is covered by the phrase '*opus Dei*'. The Rule of Benedict appears to limit it to Chapel and public worship, as in the text, 'Nothing is to be preferred to the work of God' (43.3), or that it is the abbot's care to announce 'the hour for the work of God' (47.1). Contemplative orders would follow this emphasis.

Yet what is covered by the term '*opus Dei*' needs to hear the story of Cîteaux, Burgundy. This 12th-century reform of what Benedictine practice had become restored the legitimate role of work by monks, which had become eclipsed by the alleged priority of prayer. These monks had others do all the physical work for them while they spent time in Chapel, Cell or Scriptorium. This reform also initiated agricultural innovation and change, contributing to the end of medieval serfdom and restoring physical work to being within *opus Dei*. With their application of research, experiment and study, this led to a liberation of the poor. The medieval abbey was often a centre of agricultural toil, with the abbot as its feudal lord. As such monasteries were a powerful agent stabilising and developing a Christian society.

In a similar vein, the 1934 Franciscan Rule takes a wider view and speaks of 'three ways of service': prayer, study and active work. It adds the perceptive comment that among friars there will be some specialisation, but all should include some element of each.[3]

The Celtic Rules are clear that the work of God is threefold. The Rule of Colmcille says, 'Your daily occupation should be threefold, namely prayer, manual labour and *lectio*.' The Rule of Celi De concurs: 'Each day carries with it three duties: prayer, work and reading.'[4] That text continues with the same concern about idleness. That the work was physical is clear from Ailbe 24: a bell was rung before chapel, 'so that each monk may have time to wash his hands and put on his habit'. So today, Northumbria Community leaders write that 'the work of God' includes three areas: work with mind, heart and hands, not just prayer. It is engaging the 'heart – daily prayer to nurture the soul, mind – study/*lectio* to nurture the spirit, and hands – manual labour to nurture the body'.[5] I take the threefold view.

As such, work is not just a weapon to avoid idleness; it feeds spiritual health. There are times in the Christian life when Chapel is a drudge and Cell is just empty. God has clearly gone away without leaving a forwarding address. One remedy found by the monastics was to focus on our work. Precisely when you are down is the time to keep up your rhythm of work and to be conscious of yourself doing it and focused on it. Then, as Meg Funk writes, 'Work is the back door to true prayer.' It is a friend to the soul.[6]

Garden and the focus groups

The Church Army group tended to interpret Garden as limited to its agricultural sense. They offered the following: the community's place of provision through vegetables, fruit and flowers, as well as herbs with a link to healing. They saw it as an ordered, hard-working, useful place, embodying sustenance and God's provision. Its necessary self-sufficiency could also generate income if excess produce was sold. This place of shared, physical work was also one of peaceful creativity, communing with nature, play, talk and a place to meet God. They added that one section of the garden would be a burial place, full of memories.

The Northumbria Community group came up with a definition of similar width, but made explicit Garden's complementary roles to other spaces. It is for both physical and spiritual fruit, work to sustain the community and manual work to balance the mental work of Scriptorium. It is a place of productivity and producing for others, so closely related to Refectory.

They saw that Garden embodies work as prayer, as did basket-weaving, the classic example of work in the desert tradition. Doing something practical can open the mind to God. As they put it, 'When hands are occupied, the mind is free.' At the same time, working a garden keeps you fit. They also included that the literal garden itself is a gift of God: an open, varied space of auditory and visual glory that speaks of God, with colours, air, birds and creatures. And this garden grows by itself as God intended. Pleasure is found in its beauty and bounty.

Garden and the Rules

Despite the priority of prayer, Benedict was positive about work: 'When they live by the labour of their hands… they are really monks' (48.8). Chittister puts it neatly: 'Work and prayer are opposite sides of the great coin of a life that is both holy and useful, immersed in God.'[7] Work had a wide compass. It might be 'in the kitchen, in the storeroom, in serving, in the bakery, in the garden, in any craft' (46.1) or 'on a journey or in the field' (7.63). Benedict is also eminently practical. Tools are given to trusted brothers, in an inventory, kept clean and not treated carelessly (32.1–4). But he seeks an economic and spiritual self-sufficiency for the monastic community to prevent worldly contamination: 'The monastery should, if possible, be so constructed that within it all necessities, such as water, mill and garden, are contained and the various crafts are practised' (66.6).

Franciscans too are positive about work as service. *The Principles of the First Order*, day 20, observes: 'Active service of the Master begins within the house and garden.' This includes the menial and the manual, shared out among all, considering the interests of the community. Initially existing without property and living by begging, within 30 years of Francis' death missions to other countries had built 'specially constructed houses… and the land produced gardens and vegetables'.[8] Today the Hilfield gardens go a fair way towards self-sufficiency in vegetables and provide major work for the friars and volunteers.

The Celtic instinct shares the Franciscan love of nature[9] and oneness with the land. So the monks are instructed, 'Let him cultivate and share the fruits of the earth,' and, 'Let the brothers sew and wash.'[10] The Rules go further and discourage mendicancy: 'The life of a community free from the need to beg is something Satan detests. Begging prevents prayer and will not lead to heaven.'[11] A threefold function of work is explicit in the Rule of Colmcille: to fill their own private and communal needs, to do their share of work across the community and to help their neighbours in their needs.[12] Overall the monastic strands teach us that work is good and valuable, not to be avoided or got through as quickly as possible.

Some issues around work

If historically Garden is about manual work, service and provision for the community – not firstly about leisure and recreation – it is a mental shift to realise that today most of us will fulfil Garden neither in or for Christian communities, nor in a literal garden. Usually it is in an urban context of the world of secular employment, while a few do still work on the land. I commend this focus on the role and importance of the world of work, expressed in Mark Greene's series of books in the 'Faith at Work' series and the contribution of the London Institute for Contemporary Christianity.[13]

The role of paid work today is a complex one. Sadly, modern slavery, exploitation and crushingly boring work exist. At the same time, we have the demands of a 24/7 world, overwork, obsessive addiction to work and the issue of how much work is taken away from us by automation. So we have both people taking early retirement and other people wanting never to retire. Work is also a far wider notion than paid employment. Children have homework to do. People are said to 'work' at their hobbies. In my experience of being newly retired, I am engaged in voluntary work, more housework and more grandparenting work, as well as trying to write this book.

I add that our fixation with the pursuit of leisure, fuelled by an enormous industry to promote it, is a relatively recent one. Historically the only group in society with a problem of too much leisure was the landed aristocracy. Having ridden and hunted one day, what else was there to do? That's hardly our problem today. It's more likely that we are, like Martha, 'distracted with much serving' (Luke 10:40, ESV)

No rest for the wicked?

The genuine need for the mind and the body to rest does critique the monastic texts. Their fear of idleness was too dominant. Benedict instructs, 'If anyone is so remiss and indolent that he is unwilling or unable to study or read, he is to be given some work in order that he may not be idle' (48.3). If that seems tough, turn to the Celtic voice and you meet this: 'The measure of your work should be to labour until tears of exhaustion come.'[14] The Rule of Carthage is less extreme but does refer to 'hard work in their hands'.[15] The related Rule of the Celi De insists, 'There should be no idleness in the monastery and so instruction, writing and the repair of clothing or some other useful work should be provided.'[16] Columbanus provides a more nuanced view, advising that 'labour must be moderated', because pushing disciplines too far becomes a vice, not a virtue.[17] The critique from scripture is its positive view of rest. Foundational is the Genesis text of God resting on the seventh day of creation, thus instituting the sabbath (Genesis 2:2).

Professional, amateur and vocation

Another way to see Garden as a sacred place is through what may be new thinking to some, which is actually old. Today we obsess about standards, risks, safety and performance. In both Christian and secular society, we have elevated the word 'professional' and denigrated its contrasting word 'amateur'. The first means competent, qualified and impressive; the latter implies flawed, inadequate and sloppy. I suggest we would do better to value the word 'vocational' instead of 'professional'. Our Christian belief is that all humans are called by God to work. Our gifts and our calling are linked. Our work should be vocational, that we are called to it. That's hard for those whose work is in boring, repetitive roles, but a vocational attitude to them can be releasing. Note that the advice 'whatever do you do, work at it with all your heart' (Colossians 3:23) was addressed to slaves, and it goes on to say, 'as working for the Lord'. We need to rehabilitate work in the spirit of George Herbert's hymn 'The Elixir': 'Who sweeps a room as for thy laws makes that and th'action fine.' Here the delight lived by Brother Lawrence doing menial work in his kitchen is a beacon of hope: 'In the kitchen, to which he had a strong natural aversion, he trained himself to do everything for the love of God.'[18]

All Christians are especially called, for even becoming a Christian is vocational. As Jesus said, 'You did not choose me, but I chose you and appointed you so that you might go and bear fruit' (John 15:16). Our vocation applies to who we are, to our working lives (paid or unpaid) and to our family life, not just to our church roles. Having work, works; it is how humans work best. That's why idleness and unemployment are so destructive. If vocation were central to our understanding, we could recover the loveliness of the word 'amateur'. From its Latin root *amo* – to love – it means doing something for the love of it. In that sense, I hope we are all amateurs.

Mind the gap

This positive and inclusive view of Garden or work is different from a gap that frequently occurs in congregational life. Our jobs, our working roles, barely get their head in the door of its worship. The exception is some intercessions. But for some reason, they tend to name only politicians, teachers, medics and the military. What about civil servants, business people, entrepreneurs and those who work in the media, legal system and social services?

In the Deal parish, we tried to remedy that by having an annual 'Work Sunday', when everyone could bring up and place on the Communion table an image of the work they did. I put my diary there. You may have other ideas of how we bring back Garden into church life. Garden must be more culturally reconnected to the vocational world of work, not limited to better care of the graveyard or having a better flower rota.

Learn from gardening

This chapter could be in danger of excluding the literal garden. Gardening itself has positive features to teach us about life. Its year reminds us that there are seasons; we cannot live in a perpetual spring of unending growth. For the same reason, gardening needs patience; it is no good shouting at a plant to grow. Disappointment is part of life; not everything planted flourishes – except weeds. Deeper in, we are co-dependent on the land and part of the very Earth, not separate from it. Strenuous response to and concerted action about our ecological crisis are vital. And deepest of all, the world is God's and we hold it in trust.

Application questions

- What would you say is the point of work?

- At your stage of life, what 'work' do you think God is calling you to?

- Explore whether you can see your work as a 'vocation'.

- How might you begin to learn the attitude of Brother Lawrence?

- How well does the balance of 'work, rest and play' get expressed in your life?

- In what ways should a Christian respond to the ecological crisis?

- How could your church help its members celebrate the role of work – and not just paid work?

✤ 8 ✤

REFECTORY
food and hospitality

The heart of community?

It is logical, not just alphabetical, to consider Refectory after Garden. Without Garden, there would be nothing to put on the table. Without Refectory, workers would not be nourished to occupy the other six places well. Refectory is the feeding place. It beats at the heart of community and nourishes it, both literally and socially. Refectory also extends community by providing hospitality. We eat, we meet and we greet, and people begin to belong. Food is not just basic to life; it is basic to a common life or community.

I am old enough to remember that it would be shocking to consider having drinks in church. I am still around to notice it is now weird not to be offered one. If we had listened to the monastic story of Refectory, we might have introduced that social and very human element of food and drink earlier into church life. It's an example of the truth that church isn't just Chapel or public worship; it is all the different places together which make church.

The focus group comments

This area was immediately and intuitively understood by both focus groups, perhaps as food and communal eating is so basic to life.

Both groups named a wide range of roles. Physically, the refectory nourishes and warms. Socially, it is hospitable, through welcome, gathering and serving. At the personal level, in meeting there can be conversation, light or deep, listening in silence and getting to know people better. All these can have missional impact.

Northumbria Community added the image of being at home and the family-like roles of recitation of group history and telling stories. They highlighted listening as well as speaking and a chance to repair relationships, saw overlaps in thanksgiving with the Eucharist and pointed out the warming role of laughter. This place is vital to the depth of community and to the informal socialisation of new members. Northumbria people had also learnt that being by the kitchen Aga was a tacit signal of being open to talk, especially in the evening.

I think it is no accident that the Northumbria Community mother house is defined as 'a resident new-monastic centre offering home, chapel, workshop, school, retreat facilities, as a sign and representation of the monastic and missional values of the Community'.[1] This order of words suggests that 'home' comes first. Every time I stay there, it is clear that the emotional and social centre of the site is its kitchen/dining room, called Brigid after her notable hospitality.

An unusual but significant place

Refectory is also relatively unusual among the other places. A bit like the famed Mars Bar, it combines work, rest and play. Work is in both the preparation and the serving of the food, not to mention the washing-up. As an unnamed nun remarked, 'Today I learned that the kitchen is not about food, but about charity.'[2] By charity she meant love. Rest is demonstrated in that we sit or even sprawl; we chew the fat; we relax. It is a break from what else we were doing. And at meals we play. How many jokes occur at mealtime? How much of the teasing in a family happens then? How many 'do you remember when' stories get told?

Historically, in northern Europe, the refectory was the warmest place in the monastery, as was its adjacent kitchen. In winter even today the refectory, because of its cooker, is the space of physical warmth compared with other rooms. Is that partly why both families and guests who are not being formally polite gravitate to a kitchen/dining area? Have you ever thought that Christianity was originally a domestic faith? The earliest churches were in a home, or even in tiny tenements, an even smaller domestic unit. The most famous example of worship in the gospels was in an upper room and known as the last supper. Is this dynamic near the heart of church – being a Jesus-focused community around meals?

This perspective has enormous implications for all expressions of church. I am now convinced that the 'church = Chapel' equation is a false one, not because it has no truth, but because Chapel has eclipsed many other legitimate functions of being that my study of monasticism has unwittingly unearthed. Going further, the advent of fresh expressions of church has placed significant questions over whether the process of starting a fresh expression of church or church plant should begin with public worship.[3] There is increasing evidence that the foundation of being Christian is being community centred around Jesus. Public worship is the consequence of this reality, not its creator.

Refectory in the Rules and in scripture

In the Rule of Benedict, Refectory is given the most treatment after Chapel (see 31, 35, 36, 38–41, 43, 53, 56). Indeed, lateness at either place is particularly frowned upon (43.4ff, 43.13ff). Even today, being late for a meal is not good. Moreover, brothers being disciplined for serious faults are excluded from both and must eat separately. This discipline indicates a break in relationship and is invoked to induce godly sorrow. Worship and communal eating seem to be the twin centres of life. Chittister ruefully says, 'If we refuse to learn from the community… we… should be suspended from participation in it.'[4] I recall in family life naughty children being sent to their rooms without supper. The dynamics are similar.

The Rule is specific about the people who make this function happen well. It begins with the qualities of the cellarer,[5] who was in charge of provisions, equipment and the cooking (35.5, 10). He is to be 'wise, mature in conduct, temperate, not an excessive eater' (31.1). He cares 'for the sick, children, guests and the poor' (31.9). He will 'take care of everything', treating all 'utensils and goods of the monastery as sacred vessels of the altar', which at a stroke demolishes any spiritual/secular divide (31.3, 10). In a part of the Rule reverberating with awareness of the quirks of community, calmness is desired and the cellarer is urged not to 'annoy the brothers' (31.6, 17).

In addition there are kitchen servers for the week. In our culture of being served by others in cafes, fast-food outlets and restaurants, Benedict insists community works because this role is shared by all, prayed for by the rest and done on a weekly basis, in order to serve all (35.15–18, 35.1–2). Chittister underlines the point: 'If we do not serve, we are, at best, a collection of people who live alone together.' She also points out that in historical context it was men being told to do women's work so that they 'could know what it takes to spend their own lives to give life to the other'.[6] Having spent weeks on end serving in monastic communities, I take the point. Lucy Moore, connecting the seven sacred spaces to the multiple spaces in Messy Church, puts in a plea that the kitchen and its workers count as much as the Refectory (see chapter 14). All cooks concur.

Reading, from scripture or devotional books, also happened at meals. The reader of the week, because of this important role, asks the community for prayer against vanity: 'Lord, open thou my lips' (38.2–3). It is disputed how much such reading is still followed; Chittister thinks it has gone, while Abbot Jamison maintains it continues. My own SSF experience is that it was normal when I first visited in the 1960s, and now it is occasional during the week, with silence only at breakfast. Perhaps the latter mixture adds richness and assists spiritual awareness, and less frequent content makes it easier to attend and apply what is heard.

The refectory was also a focus of ministry to guests. 'Guests… are to be welcomed as Christ', as are 'poor people and pilgrims' (53.1, 7, 15). They are met by the superior and all the brothers and prayed with (53.3–4). Yet the guests are not seated among the brothers as a whole (53.8). Benedictine scholars have long been divided on interpreting whether the Rule meant a separate room or a separate table within the one room.[7]

Chittister illuminates this sixth-century context, noting that in the collapsing culture of the Dark Ages, the monasteries became the hotel system of Europe. Benedict says of guests that 'monasteries are never without them', so two brothers were assigned yearly to this role (53.16–17). With so many travellers passing through, the need for some separation of brothers and guests arose. Chittister writes, 'We all have to learn to provide for others while maintaining the values and structures, the balance and depth, of our own lives.'[8] I noticed the same in Taizé, with the brothers having a firm practice of periods of the day apart from the presence of the thousands of young people. The Northumbria Community house team agrees. They provide this by the quiet hour after daily midday office, days off and short periods when the house is closed.

The subject of food is also covered by Benedict. A summarising comment from an abbess is that 'the fare will always be ample and will always be simple but pleasing. These were working monastics who needed energy to toil and peace to pray.'[9] Moreover, quantities could be changed if climate, heavy work or fast days required it. Because of that variation, Benedict knew it was important that recipients did not grumble (40.8–9). In our society, where food is more plentiful, exotic and varied than ever, that last word is apt.

The Celtic sources have similar things to say about the importance of the refectory,[10] cooks and food. The housekeeper knows that 'the quality of food will greatly influence the standard of observance'. Ailbe says they need a cook who is 'generous, fair and strong', providing 'water, bread, salted or fresh meat, ale curds or fresh milk'.[11] The cook should be of 'a generous and hospitable temperament'.[12] The hospitality to be provided is charmingly detailed: 'Let there be a spotlessly clean house, with a good fire therein for the guests. Let foot-washing and bathing facilities be provided for them together with a comfortable bed.'[13] It all makes sense, though we need a contemporary translation of foot-washing.

The 'repast should be of moderate measure'.[14] 'The essential thing for the refectory... is that a substantial meal be provided for the workmen wherever they may be.'[15] In the end, the matter is as much about the attitude of serving out of genuine humility and hospitality; the questions of quantity and quality derive from that. Then our refectories will nurture community, not merely fill stomachs.

I leave the last word in this section on Refectory and monastic communities to Jamison. Reflecting on two of the three words in their vow of profession, he suggests that 'fidelity' is but one translation of the Benedictine phrase *conversatio morum*. He connects it to the oldest and now obsolete meaning of the word 'conversation', which is 'living with somebody'. So he thinks 'this Benedictine vow is a resolution to live with others'.[16] Sitting round the table of the family is where this is made very practical, but also even iconic. 'Stability' in the Rule of Benedict is related to resisting the temptation to think the grass is greener elsewhere, shown both by its first chapter, which condemns wandering, critical monks called 'gyrovagues', and by the closing chapters, which focus entirely on community relations. 'Benedict is clear that you can only grow in the spiritual life by staying not so much in one place but with one stable community.'[17] Those we regularly eat with are those we tend to stick with, and vice versa.

It is almost unnecessary to add well-known biblical material about the importance in Middle Eastern culture of food and hospitality. I give a few examples if readers want to refer to them: in the Old Testament, the hospitality of Abraham to his three surprise visitors (Genesis 18) and the sacrificial provision given to Elijah by a widow at Zarephath (1 Kings 17); in the New Testament, Jesus is often eating with others as a guest, and he hosts the last supper; Acts 2 sees the early church breaking bread in their homes; and Hebrews 13:2 urges hospitality to strangers, thereby entertaining angels unawares.

Host or guest

Jesus' example helpfully opens up the positive role of being a guest, not just a host. There is a shift in western mission today. We are used to being hosts. We put on events, where we are in control, to which we graciously invite others and give them quality hospitality, hoping they will join us. We are beginning to learn that, in a society suspicious of control exercised by others, of which the church is seen as an example, we may have to begin by being guests at their parties, in the environments they call 'home' and where we feel we are 'playing away'.

Instead of being those who spiritually have it all, we need to learn to be ready to receive, as well as offer, hospitality. Both are about more than who provides the food. Perhaps inner hospitality is about finding inner space for other people, even when it is inconvenient because we have other priorities or plans. In that loss of our freedom, a freedom to give and receive in the relationship may emerge. Mary the mother of Jesus was declared 'blessed' in her loss of control and the unexpected willing hospitality she gave to the Son of God as an embryo. Our Christian journey also means opening the door to the Jesus who knocks. He comes in to eat with us and we with him (Revelation 3:20). We begin as hosts and find we have become guests of the true host, which changes everything. Hospitality is full of surprises.

We are catching up

I have noticed over the past 40 years that in any reordering of a church building where there isn't a kitchen, one is often added, whether an actual kitchen or a functional equivalent. Moreover, the majority of the young churches that have grown up in recent years, which has been the subject of my research for over 20 years, have made food part of their communal life and their gatherings. Someone said, 'Every growing church does food, though not every church that does food grows.' Our Church Army research into all known fresh expressions of church across half of the Church of England dioceses showed Messy Church and cafe church were the two most frequent choices made.[18] Both are serious about Refectory. For them, community through hospitality is intrinsic to being church.

Thus in the social shapes and physical patterns of all future expressions of church, I hope we will put Refectory at the centre and have Chapel down the Cloister from it. Then our social spaces and our theology, which are being reframed in our missionary journey to post-Christendom Britain, will walk better together. It would also offer us the chance to reconnect better with that original domestic context of Eucharist, offering a homely balance to congregational experiences, which too often are complicated, ritualised and sanitised. If we start with the dynamics of Refectory, we shall be in a far better state to offer relational and authentic missional hospitality. As the Northumbria Community mother house manual says: 'We are not a guest house but a home welcoming others; inviting them to share our life.'[19]

In some monasteries, the chapel and the refectory were at opposite ends of the site. Soul and body are different, but both are necessary. It may be too neat, but suppose that Chapel and Cell assist the soul, Chapter and Scriptorium use the head, Cloister tests the reflexes and Garden occupies the hand. Then to build community, could Refectory be at its heart? Some important words beginning with 'h' fit well with Refectory: hearth, heart, home, hospitality.

Application questions

- Think about a positive, and also a negative, experience of hospitality you have known. What were the differences?
- What do you think is important in being a good host?
- What is equally important in being a good guest?
- Which do you find easier, and why?
- How much of a role does Refectory play in your local church?
- What do you think would help your church become more like a home?

✤ 9 ✤

SCRIPTORIUM
study and knowledge

What was it for?

So we come to the third element of *opus Dei* (the work of God – prayer, work and study). As with Garden, Scriptorium is a place where significant elements of its purpose and dynamic have changed over time; therefore, the original function needs restating.

To recover its meaning, the word 'scriptorium' needs unpicking. Its Latin is inaccessible to most people. Some impressions given can be unhelpful. Other people have translated it as 'library'. That sounds too much like a reference place or a source of free, easy reading. Even to call it a 'study' conjures up dusty leather-bound volumes; it sounds academic and perhaps detached. Within the word 'scriptorium' is a shorter one – 'script'. That is something written. Historically, this was the writing place, but why and what for? My understanding is that historically it was principally about passing on knowledge.

The monasteries spread, but they could only do so when they had not only more monks, but also more books: Bibles, prayer books and inspirational texts. Remember that in those centuries there was no printing, let alone information technology. The only way books could be made was to copy them by hand. This need accelerated in times when new monasteries were being started, as having sufficient books was a monastery-planting requirement.

It was the laborious, loving production of the only volumes that existed. In that sense, Scriptorium was about passing on knowledge, not merely acquiring it for its own sake. At Cîteaux, Burgundy, where there is an exhibition of earlier stages of monastic life, I could look through a door and see a monk in his white habit and black cowl sitting at an angled desktop, with quill in hand, engaged in the slow work of painstaking copying.

The Scriptorium's hand-written books resourced Chapel's need for prayer books and Bibles. Reading in Cells also needed parts of those texts and accounts of the saints for *lectio divina*. The material also served Refectory, where books were read out as people ate. The work of writing, reading and listening fuelled the overall life of prayer. Part of God's work is passing on knowledge. As such it was a kind of evangelism. One reason I am a Christian today is that others passed on to me what they knew and I didn't. It changed me.

Books' beauty or utility or...?

It is true that the books they made were often beautiful. Part of the reason for that artistic embellishment was a mark of respect for the value their pages contained. In the British Isles, the best-known examples are the Lindisfarne Gospels, in the British Library, and the Book of Kells, found in Trinity College, Dublin. Both are indeed wondrous and beautiful, but I reflect that this proper appreciation is profoundly different from letting the words of Jesus transform our lives. In the west there is a tendency to focus on cultural and aesthetic worth and to resist a focus on the spiritual message. Similarly, some people love the phrasing of the Book of Common Prayer more than the content its prayers memorably transmit. Or it is like listening to Handel's 'Messiah' and only glorying in the music with no corresponding hallelujah from the heart. I was therefore intrigued to find that there was ebb and flow of the level of artistic and decorated aspects to the books copied. At Cîteaux, I saw copies of the texts exhibiting a simplification of style brought in by Bernard of Clairvaux during the Cistercian reform. Beauty is truly lovely, but there is a time to pass through what is depicted, not to focus on it just for itself.

The focus group comments

The Church Army groups spotted the roles of studying, learning, writing and art, all of which are mental forms of work. They knew it was a communal resource centre which enabled private study, promoting research and discovery. It preserved the past and expanded the availability of knowledge.

The Northumbria Community group knew this place embodied 'study as work, be it of the Bible, tradition or culture'. Transcribing the Bible was both essential and of benefit to others. They saw learning for the writer and that the writing done enabled others to pass it on. The passing on blessed others and aided prayer, as copied Bibles and prayer books were used. They too included art, aware of the Lindisfarne Gospels, and so blessing others with beauty by creative expression. It drew on both left and right brain, the visual and the verbal. Thinking of Aidan and his twelve pupils, some of whom, such as Cedd and Chad, became missionary bishops, they added that it had a school function, teaching writing, study, craft and mental work. Beyond them, others have seen how the Celtic Church and its mission were a gift to Europe, in the so-called Dark Ages, of books and even of civilisation itself.[1]

Scriptorium in the Bible

Both Judaism and Christianity are faiths grounded in the conviction of God's historical intervention, such as in the exodus and exile, the incarnation and resurrection. From this follows both a command and an impulse to pass on the stories, orally and by writing. The belief in revelation from God carries the consequence of transmitting the content. The ten commandments and the elements of the Passover were given with the understanding that they would be passed on (Deuteronomy 4:9; 11:19). Psalm 78:1–4 commends the passing on to our children what we have learnt from our parents that God has done. In the New Testament Luke (1:1–4) tells us that he sets out an 'orderly account' to give 'certainty'. John's gospel also clearly hands on a tradition, that we too might come to believe and have life in Christ (John 20:31). Within John (5:19–30) we see Jesus claiming that the Father passes on to him what he says and does. Paul continues this flow, saying, 'What I received I passed on to you' (1 Corinthians 15:3). Later he commends a perpetual process: 'The things you have heard me say… entrust to reliable people who will also be qualified to teach others' (2 Timothy 2:2).

Scriptorium in the Rules

In coming to the Rules I looked for evidence of books, study, reading and writing, not so much the named place; the function would serve to prove the place existed. For example, the Rule of Augustine (5.38) refers to those in charge of books and says, 'Books are to be requested at a fixed hour each day' (5.39).

The Celtic witness tends to deal with a monk's qualities, not the places in which he acquires them. In various Celtic sources, however, we find plenty of reference to study. Ailbe says of the monk: 'He should be wise, studious and devout.' And the Son of God should be invoked in all *lectio*.[2] Colmcille refers to 'your daily occupation… prayer, manual labour and *lectio*'.[3] Carthage has a similar three fold path – 'We watch, we read, we pray' – and includes a further strand, 'the learned go to instruction'.[4] The related but separate Rule of the Celi De concurs. The Rule of Tallaght picks up the needs of those 'unable to read' and makes reference to 'the house of instruction',[5] a clear reference to the transmission of knowledge. The Rule of Columbanus knows one assessment of the quality of a monk is 'the depth of his study'.[6] This last quote connects to the 19th-century adage that Ireland is the land of saints and scholars. The books must have come from somewhere, and there is consistent expectation that they are engaged with.

The 1223 Rule of Francis is focused on living out key gospel text callings. It accepts the learned and unlearned, but chapter 10 advises that the 'unlettered should not be anxious to acquire learning, they should rather strive to have what they must desire above all else, namely the Spirit of the Lord and his holy inspiration'. Brother Ramon SSF expands: 'Although Francis had no taste for book learning and was always suspicious of scholarship within the Order, he loved the stories of the Round Table and of the other chivalrous romances we have referred to.'[7] He called the friars 'my true knights of the Round Table'.[8] However, within decades, learned Franciscans like Bonaventure were doctors of theology in Paris, sadly in rival schools to the Dominicans. The much-later *Principles*, day 6, refers to 'books which are necessary to the work of study'. Day 19 refers to study which will principally be of the soul's ascent to God, with *lectio divina* as a principal aid. It continues that some houses will be places of learning, with hours set apart for study and silence. The most recent Rule advises 'some hours each week'. Thus Hilfield has a library. Study forms one-third of the key tasks of a contemporary Franciscan.

There is a direct reference in the Rule of Benedict to such a room: 'During this time of Lent each one is to receive a book from the library, and is to read the whole of it straight through' (48.15). However, other elements within the Rule obliquely infer its presence. For example, the monk's standard clothing and worn equipment includes a stylus and writing tablets (55.19). A key reference is the famous comment on 'idleness' that specifies the need for 'prayerful reading' (48.1). This reading or *lectio* is expected by the Rule 'up to three hours a day'.[9]

Chittister pithily sums up the three work areas: 'Benedictine spirituality demands balance... He wants prayer to be brief, work to be daily and study to be constant.'[10] Reading is expected on Sundays, unless monks have been assigned other tasks (48.22). Benedict is clear that 'those who need to learn some of the Psalter or readings should study them' (8.3), as some texts were to be learnt by heart (12.4, 13.11). The Rule is not explicit about where daily *lectio* happens. With no cells, the early options were the Scriptorium, Refectory or Cloister. There is evidence that it was in public communal places, because to ensure this reading is done, it is inspected by seniors who 'make the rounds of the monastery'. This is to guard against brothers wasting time or engaging in idle talk, thus distracting others (48.17–18).

Clearly reading and study were an essential part of monastic life, sourced by a scriptorium. Knowledge was being passed on both to juniors and as monasteries multiplied.

Dangers and recovery for the understanding of Scriptorium

A corruption from transformation to information

Abbot Jamison argues: 'Until the twelfth century, Christian Europe saw all reading as the learning of wisdom… part of the remedy for our souls.' Its role was salvation and transformation. He continues: 'Those who founded the universities in the thirteenth century began a process which led to a different aim: they began to seek information about the world, and to analyse it.'[11] To shift from seeking transformation to acquiring information is lowering the bar. His view is that this led to an arrogant, controlling attitude, no longer a humble, receiving one; it led to so-called speed-reading, and reading merely for functional and entertainment purposes. By contrast *lectio divina* sees the text as gift; it is about slow reading.

Slow down, you read too fast
Slow reading is not unlike the slow food movement. Walking round Dubrovnik ten years ago, I was intrigued to see a signpost for the

Konoba Golden Shell slow food restaurant. The message seems to say: let's take time for what is socially and gastronomically important. My friend Jane in our local Northumbria Community group wrote, 'In slow food you do four things. You take a small bite. Secondly, you chew – a lot. Then you savour the flavours. Fourthly, you digest this food and it becomes part of you.' She likened it to four stages of *lectio divina*: reading the text, meditating on what struck you, praying through your responses and finally just sitting with God about it.

Stephen Cottrell put a pun into the title of his 2009 book about slowing down: *Do Nothing To Change Your Life*. Jamison describes slow reading as a deliberate circular rereading and listening for God, then turning to prayer using a phrase that has emerged.[12] In a world deluged with information, these considerations from the past sound important.

Try the Examen
This process from the Jesuits, otherwise called Ignatian spirituality, commends daily reflecting on (examining) the passing day but without self-condemnation. Tim, another friend, learnt that it boiled down to four questions: How content was I today? How meaningful has my day been? What am I grateful for today? How might I have changed my day? Through them we grow, probably pretty slowly, in gratitude and self-knowledge.

A stitch in time?
I'm not much into sewing, but even I know that overstitching is stronger. In sewing going forwards and then going back, before going forwards again is better. To be changed by God, why not learn to read like that sometimes? Say it's a passage of scripture. On day one read a few verses and ponder them. On day two go back over at least some of them, before reading on, and ask yourself, 'What is the extent to which I have taken yesterday's learning, and any change from it, on board?' Transformation is what counts. What has been passed on that is changing us? Here Scriptorium and Cell meet.

Information overload

Related to the first corruption is a second one. The 16th century saw the invention of the printing press. Two consequences of this were, first, liberation from church or state control over ideology and, second, a widening of who was educated; there is doubt whether the Reformation could have happened without these factors. But equally, irreconcilable differences grew up between published authors and groups formed round them. More information led to more division, even religious war, not deeper unity.[13]

In our own day, arguably a greater shift has occurred – the rise of nearly costless digital information. Now anybody can publish anything, and I suspect that too many do. Today we are deluged with information. Some people take speed-reading courses to cope. It is increasingly difficult to enable learning across specialist disciplines. More data does not necessarily convey wisdom or promote judgement.

We seem to be a society addicted to putting out and following more information through social media. We are awash with trivia, live in dangerous echo chambers, in which we only encounter views that affirm our own, and have widespread concerns about personal privacy, the use of the internet for crime and terrorism, the grooming of children for abuse and addiction to internet-based pornography. Widely dispensing information is at best a mixed blessing. Years ago T.S. Eliot lamented in *The Rock* that there was a life lost in how we live, some wisdom lost in mere knowledge, and even knowledge was being lost in bare information.

'Now I will show you a better way'
None of the previous paragraph is to demean study, to denigrate improved access to discovery, to discourage transformative learning or to dismiss greater freedom to challenge injustice and tyranny. But it reminds us that in the Christian life only certain kinds of knowledge are ultimately valuable. Slow, thoughtful, spiritual learning is about

transformation of the heart, not information for the head, for love trumps knowledge.

1 Corinthians 13 goes further and insists that in the end, it is love that lasts and counts. This is a relational quality, and the work of Scriptorium needs holding within that framework. True Scriptorium learning is ultimately about becoming more like Christ and his many virtues. In the new heaven and earth, God won't be interested in how much we know. But he is interested now in how much we are changing to become like Jesus.

Even this book is exercising a Scriptorium function. I hope and pray that others by reading it will find that their Christian lives are being changed and their church communities enriched. I dare to hope that they will never be able to see things in quite the same way again. For true knowledge transforms and leaves us positively different to what we were.

Application questions

- What do you think is the point of learning?
- What is the best Christian book, DVD, podcast, etc. that you have come across recently? How has it begun to change you?
- Choose a book that you are going to practise slow reading with.
- How do you ensure that you keep learning?
- What knowledge do you think you have passed on to others? How did that happen or how might it occur?

✛ 10 ✛

Why we learn from monasticism

Behind all this exploration of what the seven sacred spaces offer is a question that may be occurring to you. Is it helpful, or even right, to learn from the mixed story of monasticism?

Two objections to face

1 Surely the monastery is not real life

Some worry that lessons from monasticism are bound to involve a retreat from being in the world, as well as being unrealistic for the normal Christian to practise. This could make two mistakes.

First, it is an error to think that shut-away forms of monastic life, such as the Benedictine, Cistercian or Carthusian orders, are typical. Celtic, Franciscan and Jesuit strands of the monastic story deny this. They are engaged in an outward trajectory to and with the world. For them, the seven spaces were not so much shapes fabricated in stone as portable mental furniture to live out in daily life. Ray Simpson, writing on what he calls Celtic people's monasteries, notes:

> They served as prayer base, drop-in centre, library, school, health centre. They offered soul-friends, training, entertainment and work to local people… Children, housewives, farm workers and visitors would wander in and out and worship together.[1]

Second, we should not ignore that the original calls to the monastic life were about what deeper life in Christ is about for everyone. I develop in this chapter why God raises up such groups to renew the life of the rest of his church. At best the monastic life is not about spiritual elitism, though that is a danger. Just as Formula One racing has led to more efficient engines and better brakes and tyres in everyday cars, so monastic life was intended to be a way to raise the quality of the whole church.

2 Monasticism was discredited at the Reformation

Luther, then an earnest Augustinian monk, found that, try as he would, he could not keep the Rule. His conscience nagged him, and God's justice condemned him. Probably in 1512, he 'suddenly felt the force of the text, "The just shall live by faith."'[2] From scripture he discovered that following the justifying Christ was for all. Trying to live the life of the monk could not confer merit or salvation, which was only by the grace of Christ, received by trustful faith. More than this, leaving the cloister underlined a reality: 'The only way to follow Jesus was by living in the world,' in one's daily vocation.[3]

A Lutheran, Dietrich Bonhoeffer, wrote about costly and cheap grace in the late 1930s. He held that free grace alone saves, yet it is costly because by it one becomes an earnest disciple, which costs everything. He is equivocal about the value of monasticism. He praises the astuteness of the church after Constantine in 'finding room for the monastic movement', keeping the older vision of costly grace alive. He calls it 'a living protest against the secularisation of Christianity and the cheapening of grace'.[4] The problem was this path became seen as an achievement of the elite that the laity could not emulate. By allowing specialists, it justified low standards for the majority.

The dissolution of the monasteries under Henry VIII was partly because they had become rich and corrupt. Legal processes between 1536 and 1541 disbanded 900 monasteries, convents and friaries in England and Wales. Following his 1534 visitation programme, Thomas Cromwell superintended, through the 1536 Court of Augmentations, the appropriation of their income and assets, though providing pensions for some of their 12,000 former personnel. Initially envisaged as increasing income for the crown, much monastic property was held and then sold to secular landowners to fund Henry's military campaigns of the 1540s. Only 15% of this wealth went back, as had been promised, into cathedrals, colleges, provision for the poor and the creation of grammar schools.

Dissolution was plausible because of long-standing wider dissatisfaction across European society. The call for reform of the Church across Europe was more about 'administrative, legal or moral reformation; hardly ever of doctrinal reformation'.[5] Scandals, injustice, incompetent, unlearned clergy and inefficiency were all known problems. The period also saw the rise of a wider educated class able to read the Bible and stories of the more impressive early church. Erasmus wrote satirically about the corrupted church, lowering 'the reputation of popes and clergy, monks and friars and (above all) of the theologians'.[6]

The story in England is that the monastic houses controlled 40% of parish appointments and 25% of the nation's landed wealth. There was also widespread prejudice, not least since the days of Cardinal Wolsey, against any control of society in England by an Italian pope. In addition there was an abused parallel legal system of church law and courts which made clergy and monks almost legally untouchable, but which enabled them to prosecute the laity. Too many monks were in practice idle, slack about prayer, self-serving and detached from helping ordinary people. Some were given to vice; others were well off through income from land, tithes, veneration of relics and pilgrimages to view them. Also the Renaissance had greatly widened who had become educated. Both independent thought and their reading of the Bible in English led people to question many monastic practices and superstitious beliefs.

Reactions to dissolution were mixed: from glad concurrence, sadness at the loss of sources of hospitality, schools and charity, to revolt in the north. The leading objectors of the 1536 Pilgrimage of Grace were executed. Similarly those abbots refusing to surrender their houses were treated as traitors and executed. What began looking like reform turned out to be systematic extinction and demolition. The exception was the hundred or so abbey churches that also acted as a parish church.

The monastic story is undoubtedly tarnished, but then so is the story of the wider church. Yet the very word 'tarnished' speaks of the degrading and dulling of something that was attractive, bright and valuable, like silver. What is tarnished needs cleaning, not necessarily throwing away.

Today's decline and the reimagining of monasticism

The 19th century saw a renaissance of monastic orders, both for women and for men, as part of the Anglo-Catholic revival in Britain, which has lasted until today. My own uncle Maurice became a lay Franciscan brother in the late 1950s, after the untimely death of his wife. He worked at the mother house of Hilfield in Dorset, where I stayed with him as a teenager, and then in Plaistow in east London until his death in 1980. However, for many decades these 19th-century orders have been in numerical decline; newcomers have not replaced the numbers of those who have died. Some orders have died out and their houses closed.

What has not declined is membership of third orders; that is, those identifying with an order but wishing to apply it out in the world. This distinction ties in with the insight from Christopher Donaldson, writing an affectionate life of Martin of Tours. He argues that the root of the vows of poverty, chastity and obedience was something Martin took from his former life as a Roman soldier.[7] If so, it is possible to see these vows as only a contextual expression of following in Christ's army, but not necessarily the only way full-time service to our Lord must be expressed. It raises whether being single and without personal possessions are utterly necessary to being monastic. All the new monastic groups I am aware of, and the third orders within Franciscan and Benedictine life, gladly give place to married people and recognise that patterns of authority and economic life have changed.

Beyond the traditional monastic orders and their third-order derivatives, a new development is a number of groups broadly called 'new monastic', which have grown up in the British Isles since the 1980s.[8] I introduce some related to English Anglicanism.

One is the Community of Aidan and Hilda, begun in 1994 by a group of people, including Ray Simpson, Russ Parker and Michael Mitton. Its purpose was 'cradling a spirituality inspired by the Celtic saints'.[9] With 13 regional groups across England, today it describes itself as worldwide and ecumenical, valuing the sacramental, biblical and charismatic, as did the Celts. Ray Simpson has written a history of the community, and there is a website with resources.[10]

There are also three loosely connected groups, each relating to its diocese. The Community of St Chad in Lichfield, founded in 2012 by Philip Swan and Barry Wilson, looks back to Chad, the seventh-century Celtic missionary bishop of Lichfield. It has a geographically dispersed membership united by a common commitment to a spiritual lifestyle, shaped by what they call the five rhythms of grace and by participation in a spiritual companionship group. The five rhythms cover being transformed to Christlikeness, being open to the Spirit, making time to pray and read, being a positive presence in the world and sharing one's faith.

Peregrini, a community of prayer and mission, exists in Manchester diocese. It openly borrowed the Lichfield rhythms of grace but has evolved its own four forms of life, described as alone, companionship groups for 3–5, missional communities of 5–50 formed around a specific mission focus, and entire community gatherings for retreat and to renew promises. I attended its launch in September 2014.

The community of St Hugh of Lincoln, led by John Leach, sees itself as a community called to pray in, with and for that diocese. Membership is open regardless of age. The invitation is to deepen worship and prayer, discipleship and service. It was formally launched in June 2019.

Beyond these, Ian Mobsby for many years led an Alt. worship church called Moot in central London. He has written extensively about fresh expressions of church and also contemporary monasticism. Formerly he was minister of St Luke's, Peckham, in south London. Within it is the Wellspring Community Peckham, described as a diverse yet local spiritual community of people inspired to follow the example and way of Jesus, drawing on contemplative prayer practices and engaged in local loving action.

Ian has also started the Society of the Holy Trinity, of which he is now the guardian. Its strapline is, 'A collaboration of Anglican/ Episcopalian New Monastic communities.' It is a nationwide network of communities, with a calling to urban settings, who are pursuing the religious life, that is, wholeheartedly following Christ and putting the gospel into practice. They hope that by offering their lives in this way, they can act as a resource and treasure that serves and enriches the whole church.

I myself belong to Northumbria Community, which comprises about 2,000 people dispersed widely across Europe, North America and Australasia.[11] It is led by an abbot-type figure tending the life of the mother house, a second person responsible for its school for monastic living and a third person taking the lead for its dispersed life.[12] The mother house, known as Nether Springs, is some miles inland, south of Lindisfarne. The community takes its inspiration from the saints of the seventh century, like Aidan, Cuthbert and

Hild, but traces those roots back through the Irish church, the Desert Fathers and eventually to the apostle John. It is post-denominational, with Anglican, Catholic and Baptist founders. The rule boils down to two key words: 'availability' and 'vulnerability'. These cash out in relationships with God and others. That in turn is related to two intersecting words, 'monastery' and 'mission'.

The Order of Mission (TOM) is found in several countries. It was officially launched in 2003, when the first novices took vows. TOM coined a contemporary translation of the classic vows of poverty, chastity and obedience, as simplicity, purity and accountability. The purpose was founding missional communities to work with young adults and to pioneer small-sized fresh expressions of church. Its central disciplines are a set of eight teachings called 'life shapes' and promoted by a related organisation called 3DM. The founder was Mike Breen, then rector of St Thomas, Crookes, Sheffield. By then based in the United States, he stepped down as leader and senior guardian of TOM in 2015. Some have found the life shapes and the support of accountability groups, known as huddles, very helpful. Others question the high cost of 3DM training and doubt the biblical basis for life shapes, their mechanistic feel and the fact that they do not help people cope well when life is difficult.

Many of these groups are only known to some or locally. I fully expect there are others, not least those in other denominations, that I am not aware of. Yet even what is listed here shows something of significance is happening. At the 'Religious Life and Renewal' conference at Lambeth Palace in 2014, Archbishop Justin Welby said, 'I cannot easily find an example of a church that since the end of the Roman empire has found renewal without there being flourishing religious communities.' He went on to trace how often that has been true.

Why has the 'new monastic' arisen?

Creating communities of resistance

The first fruits of the 'new monastic' emerged in several founders and the communities they birthed, which broadly share a context: Bonhoeffer and Finkenwalde in the 1930s, George MacLeod and Iona Community in 1938[13] and Brother Roger and Taizé from August 1940. They have in common a background of war or its threat. I wonder whether they are all communities of resistance – countercultural signs of alternative ways of living. The particular charism[14] of Taizé, which is reconciliation, is highly apt in time of conflict.

Resistance is an early Christian feature. Rowan Williams, in *Why Study the Past?*, points out that the early Christians were odd. They believed they were a new version of the human race, with exclusive claims to the loyalty of their members. This stood against the sacred reality of empire and the unifying venerating of the emperor, a system claiming to be ultimate, holy and with legitimate power. By contrast, the Christians called themselves holy, or saints. They met in *ecclesias* (gatherings of voting citizens), so they claimed a citizenship of something and, as *paroikoi* (immigrant workers), their loyalties were somewhere else. So martyrdom narratives become their characteristic form of writing and mutual recognition between churches. This heroic act affirmed that the empire could not have the last word, for another king was acknowledged, especially in death, as an act of resistance. Williams also comments, 'It is still true that the Church will at times find its unity when it finds what it has to resist.'[15]

There is a danger of focusing too much on resistance and only finding a unity in what is opposed. Such negativity is not the same as the early-church dynamic of belonging to an alternative kingdom and its sovereign. Then the stance taken springs from divinely bestowed internal identity, not secular external threat. I suggest today's monasticism is seeking resistance to today's dominant powers.

Venerated and supposedly unifying idols today might be economics, consumerism, individualism, entertainment, nationhood or sport.

Another strand of resistance is seen in Jean Vanier and the L'Arche communities beginning in 1964, in which so-called handicapped and equally so-called normal people live in community, thus refusing to find value only in the ostensibly beautiful and intelligent. Recemt disclosures about Vanier stain his reputation, but not these values. In later life, Henri Nouwen joined them and is eloquent about the brokenness of us all.[16] I now think the personal discovery of a blessed frailty is one enduring strand of the monastic, from the Desert Fathers onwards. Francis in particular lived out humility as the joy of dependence and surprised acceptance, redeeming humility from the self-deception of exaggerated self-denial.

Arguably consumerism could be a leading candidate to resist. It combines materialism, hedonism and individualism. It has its own enormous evangelism budget called advertising. Its message is encoded in the language of rights, especially of choice. Its vocabulary and plausibility are already powerful. Its knock-down arguments cite phrases like 'but the bottom line is', and people already speak of 'buying into ideas'. 'Retail therapy' may have a short-term buzz, but it is no therapy towards health. It is designed to be addictive by stimulating our desires and intentionally not fulfilling them on a long-term basis.[17]

Embodying the repudiation of excess

It is said that the boomer generation, growing up since World War II, has been the most affluent in history. Consumerism could only flourish in a sufficiently widely wealthy economy. I wonder if the rise of new monasticism is part of a countercultural protest. I want to qualify the word 'protest', because it sounds like standing on the sideline and hurling abuse. I mean rather the protest of passive disobedience to norms around us and choosing a lifestyle that raises its own questions of the culture. As Benedict puts it in his Rule, 'Your way of acting should be different from the world's way; the love of Christ must come before all else' (4.20).

In the face of this, vows like poverty and values like self-denial are so crazy as to attract attention for their sheer difference. Only as people are transformed by Christ, caught up in the God-given delight of loving God, confessing, and facing and repudiating their addictions, can new attitudes grow. These I believe would be attractive to others. We need to become noted for our spirit of giving and generosity, as an overflow of spiritual life within.

Some earlier monastic foundations, like the Franciscans and the reform of Benedictine practice by the Cistercians, occurred in periods when the rich and poor were sharply contrasted. So the Rule of Francis is based around three New Testament texts that emphasise the self-denial that leads to life, through selling possessions and giving to the poor. Yet this resistance to secular excess is not the only factor. We should link it also to a high level of dissatisfaction with our spiritual life and the way the consumer virus is virulently present in the church.

At best, new monasticism repudiates several excessive elements and points a way forward:

- a protest against excess by choosing to live the value of simplicity.
- a protest against the addictive perils of possessions by embracing poverty.
- a fast from the assault of information by daring to enter silence.
- a renunciation of obsession with sex in the welcoming of chastity.
- a rebuttal of isolating individualism through embracing the demands of community.
- a blessed relief from the curse of being driven, through finding a sense of balance.

I myself value a new centre that has a higher power to challenge my own addictions. I can see how I can be a driven perfectionist. I can see ways in which I could be an addict in need of help. As a consumer, I confess to enjoying the three successive BMWs I have owned, and I need discipline to only play the number of computer games that are a good break. When I was still employed, I knew what it was to work over-long hours and had to learn to say no to speaking invitations by making myself accountable to my team over any requests that came in. I may have further addictions that my wife knows better than I do.

Calling for clarity in an indistinct church

One way the church creates a habit of being indistinct is by being satisfied with church attendance as an adequate mark of being a disciple. Wider church features that collude with this choice are the collection of church-attendance statistics and the assessment of financial dues using that basis. Mere attendance has all kinds of damaging influences:

- It reduces community, because people scoot off as soon as the service ends and don't mix.
- It stifles lay ministry aspirations, because being there is enough.
- It colludes with clericalism and lay dependency that thinks, 'Father knows best.'
- It fits with 'our right to have a vicar to do services for us' and can drift towards the 'my church that I don't go to' mentality.
- It reinforces the passivity that pew-sitting can create.
- It allies today with consumerism. There are too many Christians who demand to be 'fed', but seem averse to learning, as opposed to teaching, and so don't grow as disciples.
- It buttresses over-investment in church buildings.

Archbishop John Sentamu said in his 2005 enthronement speech: 'It is a scandal that many Anglicans are consumers of religion, not disciples of Jesus Christ.' In the church that is emerging, attendance will not be enough. Discipleship is crucial, and I explore this further in chapter 13. All the new monastic groups, from the 1930s onwards, stress this.

How sad that there is still too often a basis in the old charge of hypocrisy. What a contrast to the practicality and the attraction of what Jesus commended: 'Let your light shine before others, that they may see your good deeds and glorify your Father in heaven' (Matthew 5:16). At the close of a story about his parish discovering a monastic calling, Hugh Ellis remarks, 'Throughout history whenever the Church has become slack in its distinctiveness, monastic communities have arisen.'[18] Williams, unpacking the beginnings of the Desert Fathers and Mothers, sees it as the search for clarity:

> The early monks and nuns moved off into communities of the desert because they weren't convinced that the church in its 'ordinary' manifestations showed with any clarity what the Church was supposed to be about... what humanity really was when it was in touch with God through Jesus Christ.[19]

Antonio Romano, influenced by the post-Vatican II emphasis on the work of the Holy Spirit on founders of religious movements, has Pachomius (293–345) and Benedict (480–543) in mind when he writes:

> The founder has the great merit of being the one to have approached the shortcomings of the time in which they lived with ingenuity and to have tried to make up for them by personal example.[20]

The attitude among these founders is significant. Romano sees a significant difference in humility between those who act as rebels rather than innovators: 'The second works within the system, while the first leaves banging the door.'[21] In today's culture, not noted for its patience or humility in the face of the past and critical in its views of the elderly, contemporary founders in new monasticism might take note. Francis held that tension, being described as an 'obedient rebel'.[22] Yet Romano does not imply that founders are acquiescent in the face of a dull or stubborn church. Because the root of their creativity is a gift of the Spirit, they may be 'unexpected and daring'.[23] As vanguards of the Spirit, their charism keeps 'them moving ahead of the Church. They are placed like a sign of contradiction for all those not living their Christian lives urgently.'[24]

Romano knows the genuine originality of the founders can be disturbing and cause difficulties to the Church. Yet they are to be seen as prophetic, not heretical. They question some aspect of the Church, but do not call into question the Church itself. As such, they resist the temptation to become gnostic; that is, seeing themselves as recipients of a privileged esoteric wisdom while those outside are dismissed as benighted.

One contemporary voice calling for necessary disturbance, as it happens in the Roman Church, is Gerald Arbuckle of the Society of Mary. He brings insights from anthropology on how societies change and resist change. He is concerned that the hopes of Vatican II have not been realised, and acts as a consultant to religious communities internationally. In his book *Refounding the Church*, Arbuckle notes that 'religious life historically flourishes at time of corruption with Church and society', but he thinks that today they are 'not exerting the shock effects with the Church that their vocation demands'. Too often there is rhetoric but not action, so that they truly become desirable 'islands of apostolic creativity and prophetic witness'.[25]

Earlier, in 1930s Germany, Bonhoeffer saw similar calls and limitations in the German Church:

> The renewal of the Church will come from a new type of monasticism which only has in common with the old an uncompromising allegiance to the Sermon on the Mount. It is high time men and women banded together to do this.[26]

These interactions point out sharply long-standing questions of the overlapping relationship between a religious order and the Church, to which I return. Roman Catholics have more experience of this disturbance as a positive influence. They have lived longer with its complexity and have a higher view of the Church that reaches more easily beyond immediate conflicts. They have a strong view of the Church being one, yet to which non-heretical variants such as the orders belong by definition.

Revealing hope shining in a new dark age

I have been surprised to find a breadth of sources chiming in with this view. The saving influence of Benedict[27] is explicitly in mind in the words of Alasdair MacIntyre, the moral philosopher:

> What matters at this stage is the construction of local forms of community within which civility and intellectual and moral life can be sustained through the new dark ages which are already upon us… This time however the barbarians are not waiting beyond the frontiers. They have already been among us quite some time and it is our lack of consciousness of this that constitutes part of our predicament. We are waiting not for Godot but for another doubtless very different St Benedict.[28]

I doubt whether mere civility and intellectual and moral life will be enough, but if they bubble over from an inner life in God which transforms us to love and respect each other, I see their value.

Ian Bradley, writing about what we can learn from the Celtic Church, beyond unfounded romanticism about it, makes a similar claim about our context: 'It is most definitely a vision we need to recapture if Christianity is to shine again in our own perhaps even darker age.'[29]

We have seen the same dynamic in the call of Francis amid the inequalities and divisions of an emerging merchant-driven capitalism, together with 'the triumph of worldliness in the church'.[30] It led to an astonishing response in willing followers across western Europe within a few years, including England.[31]

Brother Samuel SSF expresses this link and encapsulates the positive values that will be vital:

> Monastic life may seem utterly out of tune with the spirit of our times, yet if we are entering another dark age, it may be to the wisdom of such a way the Church of today needs to turn. I sense that the renewal of both the Church and Society will come through the re-emerging of forms of Christian community that are homes of generous hospitality, places of challenging reconciliation and centres of attentiveness to the living God.[32]

In one sentence he instinctively holds together a dynamic balance of three elements: mission exercised through hospitality; quality community fashioned through recognising true reconciliation; all infused by a spirituality centred in attentiveness to God.

'Dark age' language, with its sense of alienation, of living in a more hostile environment, of existence after the ending of a period of power, influence and self-determination, is also picked up by two out of the three questions Northumbria Community identifies as core to their quest:

- Who is it that you seek?
- How then shall we live?
- How can we sing the Lord's song in a strange land?

The second question is in the monastic spirit of all who seek to live out the gospel of Jesus, but the word 'then' suggests that this task is more difficult than it used to be. The third question is taken from the exilic period. People in exile and those living in another dark age will easily have animated conversation. However, it must not descend into mutual pity or despair. Rather the centre is to be found in the God of hope, the one we seek. To him even darkness is as light (Psalm 139:11–12). He is the God of resurrection, who raised Jesus from death and who has a track record of raising up founders to create communities of godly resistance, clearer following of Jesus, good hope and authentic communal life.

How does new monasticism sit alongside existing church?

In the life of God's Church, both stability and creativity are valuable. The two are profoundly different yet need each other. An image of this relationship might be water and fire.

Water is a very stable compound. It is a building block of life, without which we would not exist. Yet it can be destructive, in the flash flood or tsunami. It can be polluted and carry disease. It can be so cold that it kills. But put fire underneath it and a cup of tea may not be far away; even a hot bath may beckon. Fire warms water up, unfreezing and enlivening it.

Fire is both utterly different and equally elemental. No sparks means no cooking. No fire means no welcoming hearth. No flame entails no central heating. It can even be used to heal. Yet fire out of control in a forest or building is terrifying; burns to the skin are seldom good and fire in an explosion is deadly. So firefighters take water to an incident to help bring fire under control, restraining its excesses and making safe its power.

God is creator of water and fire. He is faithful and he is creative. He has both elements in his Church. Like fire and water, they are different; they are both valid, and they need each other. But they do not become the other. Let me unpack the terms 'modal church' and 'sodal church'.[33]

Modal church is the more common. Like water, it is stable and settled. This way of being church sticks in an area, occupies its own space and is comfortable with hierarchy. It is exhibited by parish and diocese. It operates in procedures and regulations. It is generalist, working through familiarity and families, drawing people slowly to Christ. It tends to be soothing and undemanding; it is open to all and ostensibly easy to join. There is much good about it. The first-century church of Jerusalem is the earliest example, and much of the western church has followed that model. But what is settled can become stuck; stable can become unchangeable; all its energy can be inward, while fiercely policing its borders, defending its policies and ejecting its dissidents. It can end up as a clique and become poisonous.

Sodal church is fiery and restless. Like fire, it moves, searching out the frontiers, impatient to strike out in fresh directions. It is exhibited by missionaries and monastic orders. It operates by calling, gifting and commitment. It is specialist, calling the few out of the modal, winning quite new people to decide for Christ. It is high call, high cost, high commitment, and joining it is deliberately tough. There is much that is good about it. The first-century examples include Jesus, Philip, Barnabas and Paul. God has consistently called out sodal church to stretch beyond where modal stays put. God also raises it up to remind modal church what deeper discipleship looks like and so to renew the modal church if it is stuck, cold or frozen. It is God's fire under any water that has lost its life, and this is always both warming and intentionally disturbing. But it too has dangers: commitment can breed excess; contempt for modal church is pride; it can wear out its members and be too rigorous.

So there have always been both ways of being Church – the water of modal church and the fire of sodal church. Both stand in need of the other, yet neither can ever become the other.

The goal is neither lukewarm water nor smouldering ashes. Bring them into proximity, without mixing them; let them have a positive effect on one another and you get kettles and cooking pots, and even steam locomotives – to the joy of many clergy! When the fire and the water both contribute yet remain distinct, the result can be powerful, even impressive. We must understand that we need both in their glory, honouring each other in their difference and abilities.

Is Northumbria Community a kind of Church?

Northumbria Community is clear it is not modal church, in the sense of being a denomination or a set of congregations. In the past, it has been careful not to give offence at this point. Now two things are changing.

First, as the language changes and definitions loosen, some parts of the Christian landscape are being called church, though not a Church in the sense of a denomination or even a parish. The category 'sodal church' helps explain this. The variety of gospel pictures of the followers of Jesus or church also helps. Those like light or a city on a hill emphasise the Church as gathered, strongly visible and working by attracting others; other images of Church, like seeds, salt and yeast, work by being dispersed, virtually invisible and subversive. This variety of images and their dynamics suggest we can see dispersed monastic communities as being Church, without claiming to be 'a church'.

If we are minimalist about essential ecclesial qualities, this dispersed community is centred in Christ and following him. They have a common life. They live out something of the journeys of the classic four marks of the Church or its cardinal relationships.[34] That is, they relate to God in seeking *holiness*; they relate to one another in the diverse *oneness* of community life; they embrace the *apostolic* relationship of mission; and they know their relational debt to the church *catholic*. In terms of church practices, word and sacrament both are present. There have been baptisms, and Eucharist occurs as part of the rhythm at the mother house Nether Springs.

Second, an increasing percentage, anecdotally said to be one-third of those attached to Northumbria Community, see it as their church. A further third see Northumbria Community as part of being Church for them, blended with continuing in local congregations where they live. In addition, some in Northumbria Community come from a non-churched background, and it is the only church they have ever known. It is how they found faith. For this last group, standard congregational life, with its weaker sense of community, narrower attitude of enquiry, more anaemic worship style and disconnection from issues of life, would not be seen as a step forward. I regret the lack of spirituality in churches that creates this exodus, but I do not regret the existence of groups like Northumbria Community, which can reawaken faith and hope and, on the way, disturb past boundaries of what is Church. I see it as one example of sodal church, but not called to be modal church.

Bits of primary evidence

I wondered what recording a couple of snapshots of the possible stances people are taking these days might reveal. I had the opportunity in July 2019 to do so at two events put on in connection with Northumbria Community gatherings. The first was a day conference on the seven sacred spaces at a farm in Gloucestershire. The second was a retreat on the same topic at the mother house. I offered people five stances they might take in relation to attending a congregation and the complementary role Northumbria Community might play in their lives. I explained the options and had marked out a grid, on a nearby floor, so that people could stand in the segment that most closely expressed their position.

In Gloucestershire I had to divide the participants into two groups, recognising that some already had some level of formal connection to Northumbria Community and others were looking in from outside. Of the 34 people present, 23 were already linked to Northumbria Community and 11 were not. The two groups were counted separately and the results are shown in the tables below.

Table 1: Gloucestershire (34 participants)

Local church	Pleased by	Content with	Frustrated by	Holding on to	Given up on
Northumbria Community	Additional	Enriching	Beckoning	Major	Primary
NC members (23)	3 (13%)	10 (43%)	2 (9%)	0	8 (35%)
Others (11)	4 (36%)	0	4 (36%)	3 (27%)	0

Table 2: Northumbria Community mother house (18 participants)

Local church	Pleased by	Content with	Frustrated by	Holding on to	Given up on
Northumbria Community	Additional	Enriching	Beckoning	Major	Primary
NC connected	1 (6%)	5 (28%)	4 (22%)	0	8 (44%)

These numbers are tiny, and I cannot know if they are representative, but they act as a straw in the wind. They suggest that there is a connection between people finding congregational life no longer tolerable and positive identification with Northumbria Community. I have no way of knowing which of these two factors came first to influence the other.

They do confirm the guess that a good third of Northumbria Community adherents are no longer part of a congregation. It also underlines the low level of satisfaction with existing church. Doubtless too there is great variety, from splendid to appalling, in the quality of local churches. By no means are all of them struggling, weak or unhealthy.

What might new monasticism say to the Church?

People want a spirituality that makes sense of life and has vigorous yet achievable demands. Another way to put this is to speak of the attraction of the craziness of following Jesus seriously:

> When Jesus sent his disciples out on mission he told them to be poor and to take nothing with them. And he told them to do things that were impossible to do all by themselves. So it is for all missions. Communities and members are called to be poor and to do impossible things such as to build community and to bring healing, reconciliation, forgiveness and wholeness to people.[35]

There is a chronic need to recover rhythms beyond those imposed by the demands of work and family and the lures of leisure. The hardest rhythms to find seem to be those that will enable us to enter the domain of being alone, to seek God with attentiveness, accepting the vulnerability of that encounter. It will mean going deeper than the quiet time; I unpacked that in chapter 3. Longer rhythms will include times of self-denial, coming out of work and family, in order to take a retreat. This will be more significant than the temporary loss of chocolate during Lent.

Bradley asks, 'Could it be... people are actually craving commitment, discipline and obedience?'[36] Brother Ramon helpfully explains that such obedience should be neither slavish nor unconditional like in the military. Legal obedience may be necessary in society; however, it is but dutiful not joyful. Better is wisdom-based obedience, by which a master leads a novice into maturity or which is exhibited by a loving parent teaching discipline to a child. Best of all is loving obedience, harmonising with the will of God, joyfully perceived and assented to.[37]

Yet this obedience cannot be found alone and so links to the desire for accountable community. Being together is a gift to help us dare to be alone. The two are intertwined, as Bonhoeffer cautions: 'Each by itself has profound perils and pitfalls... Let him who cannot be alone beware of community. Let him who is not in community beware of being alone.'[38]

My own journey of the past 20 years makes me think that new monasticism is more significant than some kinds of fresh expressions, which commendably focus on connecting with those outside the church but may still be infected by society's values. If the need today is for deep people, then here is a portal – a way through and onwards – to inner attentiveness in following Jesus and the painful but liberating process of being transformed by him, in community. No other fresh expression of church can afford to ignore this strand and will be well advised to spend significant time pursuing this depth of spirituality. Only when mission meets monastery will there be balanced sustainability.

Can we learn from this source?

I conclude that the flawed history of monasticism is a cautionary tale, and we should not be naive about its dangers. Yet we are wise to take on board that the heart of monastic life is for all Christians. Third-order movements testify to this. There is a long story of God calling sodal groups of Christians, to some degree for their own sake, but principally to call the rest of his church to spiritual renewal. Such an untidy and disturbing movement is under way again. We are blessed to live in such desperate and also hopeful times.

Application questions

- Jot down a summary of your view of monasticism before you read this chapter.

- If this has now changed, in what ways? How far is your own church 'a community of resistance'?

- What do you think would help us to avoid having an addictive lifestyle?

- How can the church's image and witness best be enhanced?

- How could modal and sodal church serve each other well?

- In the grids on page 141 assessing a current stance to one's own church, which category did you most identify with?

✤ 11 ✤

The seven sacred spaces and life

Echoes in other architecture

Some may wonder if these spaces and their functions are just for monasteries. I think not. As Joan Chittister says, 'The Rule of Benedict is concerned with life: what it's about, what it demands, how to live it.'[1] That is a call to all Christians, but there is evidence that the seven spaces go further.

Cathedrals

These ancient buildings, often from abbey foundations, contain side chapels with a specialist private prayer function within the overall edifice. Cathedral sites also often encompass cloisters and a chapter house and are surrounded by, or are beside, a garden. Some have a study centre, which relates to Scriptorium, and more recently many have introduced a cafe, thus restoring functions of Refectory. Their quiet corners and their individual chairs, not pews, can act as Cell. The confessional box does link to the function of Cell, but private space is created more by the individual within the vastness of the overall complex and is not a primary function of the architecture.

Conference centres

Those such as Lee Abbey also exhibit these seven functions. I wonder if that contributes to the sense of significance that time spent there often engenders. Do the spaces, with their variety of doors to encounter with God, the self and community, provide richer ways to be Christians together, compared with the Chapel-dominated experience of much congregational experience?

University colleges

Universities with medieval foundations were perhaps unconsciously built on the monastic pattern and holistic intention. Most of the features are obvious. The Cells are the individual rooms on staircases. The Chapel speaks for itself. Chapter became the senior common room or the principal's house. Cloister and Garden are seen in the quads. Refectory is prominent, complete with high table (remember, the abbot dined separately) and younger members sitting down only when bidden. The library and tutors' studies echo Scriptorium.

Those echoes are there, but the priorities have changed. The value put on the Scriptorium has grown, in line with the 13th-century change in the understanding of knowledge, noticed by Jamison. Chapter and Refectory have become places of power with privileged dining rights, a high table and much to eat and drink. Chapel is now marginal, not central, to the life of the college. Historical independent schools have very similar dynamics.

Houses

In larger or older houses the seven can be still discerned. Bedrooms are the Cell. It is Chapel that has gone missing, although the tradition of family prayers is only a few generations dead, and through spiritual direction more people find and embellish a particular place in the home. Family conferences act as Chapter, or it happens in the parents' bedroom! The hall and landings are the Cloisters. Garden is simply the garden, often with a vegetable plot. Kitchen and dining room are the Refectory, and having a study or library is the Scriptorium. The latter may now be reduced to a computer corner. They are all there, but few know the old names. I see all this in the 1904 house I enjoy.

In a dispersed community, and in small homes, some of these places collapse into one another. Thus a prayer corner acts as Cell and Chapel, with the two weaving together. For the home maker, Refectory and Garden overlap, in that both are about work for others. Garden covers not only the green patches outside the front and back doors, but also overlaps significantly with the much wider place of work and even shopping. Cloister, in addition to the corridors of the house, can be the connecting times and transitions between work, rest and play, such as commuting. It also becomes those unplanned meetings with friends and strangers.

Yet come the modern city apartment and the denuding of this rich inheritance has gone further. At worst the kitchen has gone, with people eating out or taking fast food on the run. Living as a solitary person with an intercom to keep anyone else out robs any hall of meetings and reduces the function of Chapter to what I decide by myself. Garden becomes a window box, Cell becomes responding to digital media and Scriptorium is reduced to material from the internet.

A hint about being human

The above list of places where the seven spaces still leave the imprint of their purpose is more than testimony to an unconscious architectural inheritance. I suspect the seven spaces connect with what it is to be human. Human beings need to be alone and together. We have to make decisions. In the 'work of God', we need balance across prayer, study and physical work. We need to recharge, engage and socialise. Doing that while you eat is wonderful. Could it be that the shapes and places within the monastic tradition have a vital gift to offer to us as we struggle to know what is truly human and how best to be church?

Llandaff Diocese has helpfully taken my original seven-spaces thinking as applying to whole secular communities, not just Christian communities or secular buildings (see the story from

Richard Lowndes in chapter 14). In such a wide view mindfulness is Cell; a football match might be Chapel; the city council or boardroom practise Chapter; dog walkers, the school gate and the water cooler at work experience Cloister; orchestra and the gym are forms of Garden; the pub, cafe and canteen reveal Refectory; while Scriptorium is found across the U3A, libraries, radio book clubs and even Google.

If the seven spaces and what they enable are understood and practised, there is more likely to be harmonious balance in the whole of life, living out the dynamic of being alone and together.

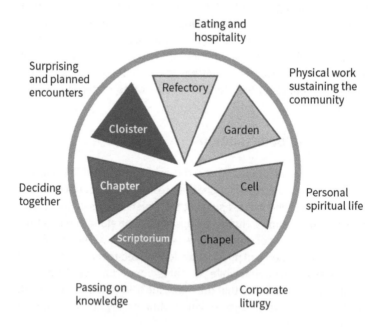

Figure 1: Seven spaces in harmony

The distortion of church as only Chapel

Now that I am aware of this rich, diverse, yet deeply rooted way of seeing and thinking, my chief sadness is the distortion that has arisen.

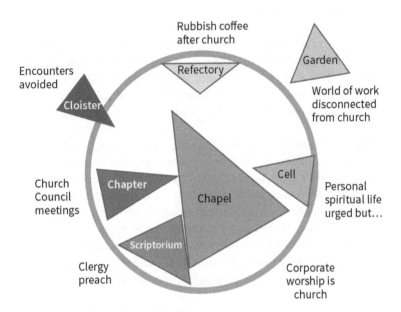

Figure 2: Seven spaces distorted

The Church has overinvested in Chapel. Instead of being one among seven spaces, Chapel occupies predominant place, at times almost eclipsing most of the others. Think how much our church buildings cost in money and time; think what ordained leaders spend their time and energy on. When people talk about 'being in church', too often they only mean entering the nave.

In such a context, Scriptorium reduces to the preacher's sermon, which we know is often a hopeless educational or transformative device. This space may rear its head as the Christian bookshop, which is becoming rarer, or more commonly those shelves of books we always meant to read sometime. Sometimes Scriptorium has been reinvented as the Bible study group, the electronic recording and distribution of sermon materials or more recently the podcast. But the historic connection of passing on knowledge that would be transformative is missed.

Chapter is narrowed to official decision-making bodies, whose reputation for Christian behaviour is not high. How many people would think that the PCC or deacons' meeting ought to be modelled on Chapter and that this too is an intrinsic part of being Church, not just a necessary evil or a legal device to control church business?

Personal spirituality is urged, but little audited. Though Cell usually happens outside the building, places for private prayer within churches are very possible. Also, all monastic groups know that being a hermit is harder and only for the advanced who have shown they do community well. It then seems perverse that the 'quiet time' tradition has insisted that Christians should begin their spiritual disciplines by living as individual hermits who are undirected. Thus the time Christians actually spend in the Cell of private prayer and being encountered by God through scripture is thin.

Other features have fared even worse. Refectory may not happen at all, or it is only that dreadful instant coffee that is mistakenly supposed to reach the parts the others cannot reach. Refectory is making a welcome comeback, as re-orderings of church premises have created kitchens and toilets, taking food and hospitality more seriously. Are they yet central enough, not merely supportive, in church life?

We do often have Cloisters, spaces between various church rooms and the walkways leading to our buildings, but I guess that they are not recognised and celebrated as such. More seriously, because the quality of much congregational community life is shallow, in-depth encounters through Cloister may even be avoided.

As for the world of work through Garden, too often it has fallen off the church agenda, and church attendance has become relegated to a leisure pursuit. Any emphasis on Garden is relegated to lawns, flowers and graves in the churchyard, while the world of work happens elsewhere.

Thus Church understood and expressed as gathered dominates over any sense of Church as also dispersed. Chapel is professionally dominated, and passive laity ensues. There is insufficient intention to pass on spiritual wisdom, and decision-making is fractious and inward-looking. Too many of us are pew-fillers but not becoming Christlike; hospitality is artificial at best and absent at worst, and the difference it makes to the rest of life is minimal. And doing Chapel better by itself cannot redress this imbalance.

The seven spaces have complementary functions that differ from one another. You now know I think that Chapel doesn't and can't do it all. I often clothe my thought in imagery. I see Chapel as being like the spine of Christian communal life, holding many things together in a quiet way. But Refectory for me is its social heart, Scriptorium its enquiring mind and Cell its spiritual soul. Make of Garden, Cloister and Chapter what you will – feet, warts and eyes?

The seven sacred spaces and natural church development thinking

I was intrigued some years ago when, while working on my understanding of the seven sacred spaces, out of the blue I received an email from a Church Army evangelist, Simon Mason, suggesting links he saw between the seven spaces and the 'eight quality characteristics' of a healthy church, taken from the work of Christian Schwarz.[2] This is his list, with him adding: 'The only characteristic I didn't match was need-orientated evangelism.'

- Empowering leadership – Chapter
- Gift-orientated lay ministry (work as service) – Garden
- Passionate spirituality – Cell
- Effective structures (the link between the eight) – Cloister
- Inspiring worship services – Chapel
- Holistic small groups – Scriptorium
- Loving relationships – Refectory

The overlaps he spots are suggestive, but not exhaustive; for example, Chapter links with both leadership and structures. Play with these two lists and see what connections you identify.

Whether there is any link from the seven sacred spaces to a clear missional aspect of being church is the topic for the next chapter. What is abundantly clear to me is that the connections made by Mason underline that the health of any Christian church has multiple elements. There is no future in relying exclusively on any single element to produce healthy Christian or human community.

Spaces and values, virtues and practices

I heard a helpful phrase recently from a former college friend about working with volunteers. He said work in any voluntary community, including congregations, needs the presence of three factors: right person, right place, right motivation. I imagine Benedict nodding his head in agreement. Here are hints of calling, context and character.

I want to protest here that church is not a business. I am among those who resist a growing managerialism around parts of church life. Yes, there might be hire-and-fire with some diocesan staff and, in extreme cases, with clergy, but essentially all expressions of local church – traditional or fresh – are groups of volunteers with very few paid staff. Here communal life is very different. How does that work? Even in monastic communities with vows including obedience, sheer compulsion is never helpful in the long term.

Jean Vanier opens up a wider perspective of what will and won't work:

> Community life isn't simply created by either spontaneity or laws. It needs a certain discipline and particular forms of nourishment. Some precise conditions have to be met if this life is to deepen and grow through all the crises, tensions and 'good times'.[3]

What are those 'particular forms of nourishment'? I find it significant that on the same page he ends this introductory chapter to his famous book on community life with a quotation from John 15. It is about love in the Trinity, Christ's love for us and his command that we should love as he does. Let me explain why that resonates for me. It connects to a sentence that I read recently in the opening chapter of Archbishop Justin Welby's book *Reimagining Britain*:

> Values guide practices, and practices build virtues; virtues also reinforce practices and guide our understanding of values. The whole process is circular, self-reinforcing for good or ill.[4]

I like this dynamic description. I agree with Welby that the circle should start with values. Vanier has named the central one at the end of his chapter: the cascade of love from the Trinity, through Christ, to us and from us. I also agree with Welby that this circle can be for good or ill. If the value was 'economics is the bottom line', we know what practices follow, but I question that such practices build virtue; rather, I see greed, envy, exploitation, fear and the pillaging of the planet. So I would rather say, 'Only good practices build virtue.' They in turn require good values as their source, such as the core one Vanier ends his chapter with.

I go further and reluctantly disagree with Welby when, a page later, he argues that 'values spring from practices of love'. It can work that way, but in Christian thought our deepest values spring from God's revelation, not our reflection or practice. This is true in both Old and

New Testaments. The inner command, which enables us to keep the other commandments, is 'Love the Lord your God' (Deuteronomy 6:5). Jesus then underlines this with his assessment of what is the greatest commandment, recorded in Matthew 22:37–39 and Mark 12:29–31, adding, 'Love your neighbour as yourself.' These values have not arisen from existing practice, but by divine command and revelation. The scenario is not like the surprise occurring in Julia Donaldson's children's book *Zog*, in which the eponymous young dragon is repeatedly helped by the practice of a runaway princess, and each time he says, 'What a good idea!' Rather, our deepest values come from above, from what is revealed of how things have always been in the loving, interdependent life of God the Trinity. We didn't invent this. It is revealed to us in Christ that God is love. This is the source and its authority. Here is where the Christian circle of values, virtues and practices starts.

Why does this link to the seven sacred spaces and monastic thought? Values, in this case the love of God and of others, begin the Rule of Augustine. Kin-love is commended in Ailbe 15; the Rule of Carthage begins with the ten commandments; and this love begins the Rule of Columbanus. The opening of the Rule of Benedict contains the sentence, 'This is advice from a father who loves you.' The essence of the life of Francis was being caught up in the love of and for Christ. All these sources are value-led. The seven spaces are then the arenas where the practices, flowing from the values, are cashed out. Moreover, we have already seen how so many of the Rules explicitly deal with fighting vices and growing virtues, a battle fought not only in the mind and soul of Cell, but also expressed in the corporate spaces. Cultivating virtues is 'a certain discipline' that Vanier named.

I have unpacked these sources to try to put the seven spaces in their proper place. They are like a theatre stage on which the practices are played out. As such, they are vitally necessary, and indeed they act as a catalyst for what lies beneath them, the growth into virtues. These in turn are but nuanced expressions of the deepest factor, which is values. The values are from above – the love of God and others. Don't expect the spaces themselves to do the spiritual work needed. But do expect them to provoke that need. Be clear what God calls communities to be like beyond them, and expect it will take the spaces to provide the practice areas. Remember the golf adage, 'Practice does not make perfect. Only good practice makes perfect.' Start with the values, know they take shape in the virtues and see them become visible in the discipline of living the seven spaces. Chapter 15 gives hints about putting this into practice.

Are there more than seven spaces?

There are more places than just the seven. Some are simply functional: lavatories, bathrooms and the dormitory were common until individual cells became the pattern. In a literal walled monastery, such as St Benet's Abbey on the Norfolk Broads, there was and still is the gate house.

Some other places I would argue are developments of the classic seven. We saw this when I included the Celtic house of instruction in the function of Scriptorium. The same principle applies by which the concept of Garden would extend to the herb shed of Brother Cadfael (of the book and TV series). It would also include the commonly occurring fish pond, mill and kiln. The commonality is the task of physical work.

The words 'hospitable' and 'hospital' are related, so the Refectory instinct for hospitality is also expressed in the infirmary or hospital, the room for sick monks (Benedict 36.7), in the named existence of the guest house in Celtic literature and maybe even in the abbot's house, though that hospitality tended to be for grandees. Other already admitted extensions of Refectory are the kitchen and the cellar.

The other space that must be named is the road or, in Celtic parlance, the coracle. By these two terms I mean when the monk or friar travels out of the monastery. I will explore that link in the next chapter on the relationship of monastery and mission.

Application material

- Use the wheel diagram showing the seven sacred spaces in balance (page 148).

- Decide which arena of life you want to apply it to. That could be your own life, the corporate life of your church or your wider community.

- Explore which aspects are well expressed and which are weak.

- It would be good to do this exercise with at least one other person, so you can compare the results – and you will find you are already doing Chapter!

- Best of all, come back to it in at least a year's time and see what has changed.

✤ 12 ✤

The seven sacred spaces and mission

Are the seven sacred spaces rather inward-looking?

Some have argued that the classic seven sacred spaces fatally lack an outward or missional component. Their focus is upon worship alone and together, on decision-making, study, meeting and eating within the community, and work to benefit it and its members. In the language popularised in *Mission-Shaped Church*,[1] the emphasis falls on *up* (worship), *in* (community) and using the resources *of* (links to the wider church), but *out* (mission) is absent.

Do the seven spaces exclude or marginalise this apostolic mark of the church? If that proves true, it would unfortunately at best support a view of church with a mission that is only attractional; in other words, the attitude and practice that says, 'We have it all; you just come to us.' What do the monastic texts and their practice have to say?

Benedict and mission

In some ways that critique does fit the Benedictine strand of monastic life. Those making this critique could quote the following:

The monastery should, if possible, be so constructed that within it all necessities, such as water, mill and garden, are contained and the various crafts practised. Then there will be no need for the monks to roam outside, because this is not at all good for their souls (66.6–7).

Moreover if monks are sent on a journey, they not only have the others pray daily for them (surely good), but on return they also come into chapel and ask the prayers of others lest they have been contaminated by this outside exposure, as the Rule or Benedict spells out (67.1–4).

Yet to be fair to its time, the Benedictine value of *stability* – that is, staying in the monastic community – was very important amid the chaos of Dark Ages Europe. They created islands of light, love, security and faith in a time when society was in the darkness of losing both hope and humane society. Their monasteries had a missional role to many guests who came to them. Not only did they act pragmatically as the hotel system of western Europe, but they also modelled a better way to live as a sustainable community. Another missional aspect was that, as their numbers grew, they kept on planting more monasteries in further places. This is a distinct missional feature.

The Celtic voices

'Celtic voices' is in the plural for two reasons. First, because there is a tension between what is said in the various Celtic Rules and the voice of history, which records a widespread practice of mission. An honours list would, in broad historical order, include Ninian and Mungo going to parts of Scotland c. 400, Patrick returning to Ireland in 432, David in Wales c. 530, Columba crossing from Ireland in 562 to Iona, Columbanus and Gall travelling to France, Switzerland and Italy from 587, Aidan leaving Iona for Northumbria in 635 and his later being called the apostle of England. His pupils included Cedd going to East Anglia in the 650s and Chad in 669 to Mercia. Those dates are significantly earlier than the various Rules, whose earliest copies are from the eighth century and are attributed to earlier saints out of respect. The Rules focus on the interior life or spiritual attitudes of the monk and some, like Ailbe, read as though addressed to one individual.

Second, I put 'voices' because there is no equivalent of Benedict in the Celtic church. There was neither a dominant rule nor even quite the same purpose. Oliver Davies writes, 'No single Rule, not even that of Columbanus, achieved supremacy, and the various foundations at different stages represent a patchwork of widely differing ascetical ideals.'[2] He goes on to explain that some lived as reclusive hermits, while others lived in communities. They are known to have had lay abbots, with their sons inheriting that role. There was also provision for both priests and bishops to have wives. Guests and strangers are well known in the Rules, as seen in the chapter on Refectory. This tradition contains a curious combination of laxity and rigour. It was artistic, ascetical and yet pastoral and communal.

A Celtic image to add to the topic of mission is the coracle. How does that fit with the seven spaces? My understanding is that the seven spaces are ultimately in your heart and your view of shared life, as you sit in your coracle, swirling and swaying, blown along by the wind, driven with the tide, following the call of God.

Francis and mission

Historically the Franciscans were evangelistic. Brother Ramon, writing of Francis' life, describes it as 'itinerant, divided between prayer and preaching'. This division elsewhere he calls living the tension between hermit and preacher.[3] There was much public speaking, with notes of peace and joy to stir up listeners to a life utterly dedicated to Jesus out of love for him. Francis saw himself as a herald, and in 1219 even travelled to meet and speak with Muslim leaders. The Rule of Francis, chapter 12, has a mission to the Saracens (no, not the famous rugby club!).

Ramon's book also tells in some detail the conversion stories of Francis and two notable followers a few decades later, Jacapone and Ramon Lull. He stresses that conversion to Christ by divine initiative, leading to a lifetime of spontaneous, even outrageous, loving discipleship, is characteristic of the Franciscan story. Even today the first aim of contemporary Franciscan tertiaries reads, 'To make our Lord known and loved everywhere.' Don't see here any division between an evangelistic focus on Christ and an ecclesial commitment to the church; Francis' 1204 call from Christ was 'Go and repair my church', leading to a 'vision of a church renewed and restored, reborn and revitalised'.[4]

Yet I confess to being disappointed that in SSF contemporary literature, the elements of the Anglican five marks of mission that are most emphasised are number four – to seek to transform unjust structures of society, including widening its inclusivity – and number five – to strive to safeguard the integrity of creation and sustain and renew the earth. The first mark, proclaiming the good news of the kingdom, including evangelism, is quite absent. Of course, marks four and five are honourable and desirable; indeed the latter is of crucial importance for the threatened life of planet earth.

I have read the testimonies of many current third order Franciscans. I found much about a healthy, sustainable balance in life: prayer and study, joy and spontaneity, spiritual direction, care of others, mutual support, acceptance and freedom, simple living, hospitality, environmental concern. These are genuinely laudable, but there was not a word about love for Christ or making him known. Moreover, in a list of suggestions to create a tailored Rule of Life, there is rightly much on spirituality, study, service and simplicity, but not a word about the mission of proclaiming Jesus.

I fear there are many other parts of today's church that find the willing and natural sharing of Christian faith not only impossible, but uncongenial and even offensive. It is seen as imposing on others. Focus group research conducted by Nick Spencer among young adults in 2003, called *Beyond Belief*, found that evangelism was seen as the second highest social sin. It was an expression of intolerance that today is, ironically, intolerable. To be an evangelist was to be beyond the pale and to be shunned by any decent, reasonable person. I have learnt through my own mistakes talking to others in the wider church that in Anglicanism there is distaste for some 'E' words: earnestness, enthusiasm and evangelism. Practise the last with either of the other two and you will meet stony silence and pursed lips and may encounter expressions of outrage. Dare to model all three and you could be in deep trouble.

Holding monastery and mission together

Northumbria Community writers pick up the tension in Francis' life between hermit and preacher. They explore the complementarity of monastery and mission through the image of the tide being in and being out. This is rooted in the geography of Holy Island/Lindisfarne and the history of Aidan settling there. When the tide is in, the island is cut off – as it were, withdrawn from the world. This stands for time alone with God. When the tide goes out, it is reconnected to the mainland. This stands for going out and serving in whatever way God calls. This prayer, and its dynamic that mission is the overflow of spirituality, is attributed to Aidan:

> Leave me alone with God as much as may be.
> As the tide draws the waters close in upon the shore,
> Make me an island, set apart,
> Alone with you, God, holy to you.
> Then with the turning of the tide, prepare me to carry your
>   presence to the busy world beyond,
> The world that rushes in on me, till the waters come again and
>   fold me back to you.

In the broad sweep of monastic history, it is possible to trace a spectrum as being from withdrawal to engagement. The desert tradition, or eremitic, explored leaving the world. The sixth-century monastic was more moderate in its demands and existed amid rural life, but the monk lived in his monastery. The 13th-century friar, or mendicant, lived out of his friary in a changing urban life, but modelling a countercultural stance. The 16th century brought the most apostolic expression, through the Jesuits and their international reach. To deeply explore this historical progression and its internal reasons, consult Gerald Arbuckle in his book *Refounding the Church*.[5]

Of course, this mission focus is not the only strand. There is still a call to contemplative monasticism for some and to being a hermit for a few. Are these non-missional? A pause for thought is that the root meaning of mission is the Latin *missio*, meaning to send. If God sends someone to the life of prayer, that is one form of mission.

Comings and goings

Sometimes in relation to mission an overdeveloped contrast between the words 'come' and 'go' has been set up: 'come' is bad and 'go' is good. The former is depicted as arrogant, self-satisfied, imperialistic and unduly controlling. Not only are such Christians held to think, 'We have it all,' but also they assume, 'To join, you will have to become just like us.' By contrast, the 'go' mentality is portrayed as humble, listening, open, courageous and exploratory. Such Christians think, 'We know the Christ we have been entrusted with, but need to discover what following him will look like in the culture he sends us to.' But are these two paths mutually exclusive? Do they point in irreconcilable directions?

I suggest the example of the divine mission in Jesus shows connections. God the Son went (that's a 'go' word) from heaven and came (a 'come' word) to earth. Within that ministry he drew others to him, famously saying, 'Come to me… learn from me…' (Matthew 11:28–29). The same gospel closes with, 'Go and make disciples of all nations' (Matthew 28:19). I suspect it is possible, even helpful, to see go and come as different stages in a wider process. Even those most wedded to the 'go' mentality will concede the attraction of Jesus and a community that looks like him. Some sort of 'come and see' is going on there. The dangers occur when those in 'come' mode close their ears to any call to 'go' beyond where they are secure, or when those in 'go' mode fail to stick around long enough for the 'come' element to take effect. Why divide what God has joined together?

A verdict

To see the seven sacred spaces as exclusively inward is to misunderstand how they work. The whole point is that they are so compelling and habit-forming that they become portable. The functions travel with us wherever we are sent. Francis himself said, 'Brother Body is our cell and our soul is the hermit who lives in it.' Thus to borrow the term 'Road' from Ian Adams' *Cave Refectory Road*, I would expect the person who has lived the seven spaces well to have them in their mental knapsack, and for each to be brought out as needed on the road. Let's keep monastery and mission connected.

Application questions

- Who are the contemplatives and who are the evangelists in your community?
- Which model of community is yours more like – Benedictine, Celtic or Franciscan?
- What would make you think your Christian community was too inward-looking?
- In what ways do you think your church demonstrates being outward-looking?
- How do you assess the balance in your own life of 'come' and 'go'?
- Scribble down some headlines of the dynamic between monastery and mission.

✤ 13 ✤

The seven sacred spaces and discipleship

A growing topic

I have lost track of how many books I have about discipleship. I have even read most of them, but sadly not consciously retained enough of their wealth. To write this chapter I dug out those that fell to my hand and wondered what they had in common.

I found two things. First, the second decade of the 21st century has seen more being written about discipleship. I don't dismiss earlier classics like Dietrich Bonhoeffer's *The Cost of Discipleship*, and another accessible modern classic is from David Watson in 1983. He wrote, 'I have a growing conviction that discipleship is one of the vital issues for today.' Pages later he went further:

> Christians in the West have largely neglected what it means to be a disciple of Christ. The vast majority of western Christians are church-members, pew-fillers, hymn-singers, sermon-tasters, Bible-readers, even born-again believers or Spirit-filled charismatics – but not true disciples of Jesus. If we were willing to learn the meaning of real discipleship and actually become disciples, the Church in the West would be transformed and the resultant impact on society would be staggering.[1]

Second, all the books pursue a question which is also a quest: what does it mean to follow Jesus Christ? Some do it through unpacking his sermon on the mount.[2] Others take Christlike virtues: Stephen Cherry explores a vulnerable humility; Rowan Williams writes on faith, hope and love and on forgiveness and holiness.[3]

What is a Christian?

If following Christ is near the heart of the matter, I wonder what difference there is between the questions 'What is a Christian?' and 'What is a disciple?' Perhaps the former is more about an identity. The latter overlaps with that, but it is also an image of a process to grow into that identity. If so, an adequate way to describe a Christian is fundamental when working out what a disciple is and how one is made. Watson's quote makes clear that being a disciple is deeper than external practices, stances in belief or spiritual experiences.

My view of what a Christian is has been sharpened in recent years by several factors. Previous answers, like being a church attender, a holder of certain beliefs, a reasonably nice person, or even all three, now seem anaemic. I have become convinced that, as Christians, our role in society is to return to being a patient, countercultural yet engaged and attractive community, in many ways like the early church.[4] The seven sacred spaces approach has provided content for that community's key relationships: with God, with one another, with outsiders and with oneself. The seven spaces help set an agenda that a community of disciples will need to work at.

What is our Christian identity? First, we are those who have been encountered by Jesus Christ. It is not so much that we found faith as he found us. He chose us before we chose him. By gift, we have become indwelt by the Spirit of God. We are those who have been caught up in the love of God – as Augustine understood and as I explained in chapter 3. Profound changes have happened to us.

The extraordinary result is that we have received a new identity. We are Christ-ians. This is talked about in the Bible in various ways:

orphans who have been adopted, captives who have been freed, spiritually dead people who have been born anew and raised to life, even enemies of God who are now his friends. All this is gift; it has been done for us and to us. In Christ, we have a new centre and new purpose. Yet it is also restoration of the initial creation. Our being in the image of God is being restored. In that sense, to become Christian is to become more truly human.

Yet two key words are missing. They are 'lord' and 'slave'. Today, the first word is only mildly troubling, though it smacks of privilege. The second is truly shocking, as we are aware that modern-day slavery exists, with its cruelty, exploitation and abuse. It should be campaigned against, outlawed and ended.

I don't write to justify that benign slavery, giving security and identity, can exist. However, I have to point out that the New Testament uses the word quite often about followers of Jesus. It appears in nine epistles: Paul, James, Peter and Jude call themselves slaves. Many modern translations shy away from it and choose the softer term 'servant'. But *diakonos* (servant or minister) and *doulos* (slave) are different words.

At the heart of Christian identity is the matter of a new belonging. The language of the lordship of Christ makes that perfectly clear. The conclusion of Matthew's sermon on the mount and a related passage in Luke 6 endorse the indissoluble connection between lordship and obedience: 'Why do you call me, "Lord, Lord," and do not do what I say?' (Luke 6:46). The monastic world behind the seven sacred spaces chimes in with this view. It is always entered by taking vows, including obedience (Benedict 58.17). This was not craven submission, but freely given death to the self. Why? Because Jesus calls us to follow him and take up our cross daily (Luke 9:23), and Paul gives the attitude beneath it: 'Obey… as slaves of Christ, doing the will of God from your heart' (Ephesians 6:6). A disciple is a willing and obedient slave who knows they belong to someone else, but equally extraordinary is learning to become like that someone else.

How then is such a disciple formed?

Unpromising routes

Sadly the meaning of the word 'disciple' has become distorted. It's based on the Latin *discipulus*, meaning pupil or student. This emphasis has pushed us towards thinking that discipleship is about learning new things or acquiring information. One route has been reliance on the sermon, in which an expert discloses their prior learning and, in theory, inspires listeners too. It assumes that an able speaker giving information leads to positive change in the listeners. The results are distinctly variable: a few are deeply inspired and changed; more love the system yet remain curiously unchanged; others merely endure it; and some even skip it. This lecture-type approach may breed preachers, but it is long-doubted that by itself it produces disciples.

A variant is taking courses. At best, this combines giving new insights with dialogue, group work, and question and answer. I noticed that Watson's 1983 book has two appendices containing a short and a long 'discipleship course'. Weaknesses of that approach include lack of preparation by course members and only intellectual engagement with the content. It's a better educational approach than the sermon, but the danger is that biblical information once more trumps character transformation. To be faithful to what a Christian truly is, we are looking for something even deeper than both sermons and courses.

Discipleship is about more than acquiring a Christian mind. It means acquiring holy habits that will involve building distinctly Christian life patterns. It will mean fighting the mental battle of abstaining from the bad for the sake of the good, in order to control desire. All serious athletes would readily understand these elements of training. It will involve immersion in prayer, study, serving, making good decisions, working, passing on the faith – all those aspects the seven spaces serve. The direction and the challenge are clear, the issue is how.

The apprentice avenue

I've started to think differently about how all this happens since learning that the Greek word *mathetes* can be translated as 'apprentice', rather than the word 'disciple'. Further people agree. Lucy Peppiatt applauds the term 'apprentice of the family business', and Stephen Cherry speaks of 'disciples as Jesus' apprentices'.[5]

A virtue of 'apprentice' is that it is a known contemporary word with energy. It immediately evokes more active and participative images than listening to sermons or taking courses. It conjures pictures of the workplace; it is about acquiring skills, learning by doing, all in relationship with a master craftsman. It moves away from formal education or merely gaining information. It is not a guru-to-devotee, dependent or sycophantic relationship sometimes evoked by the word 'disciple'. In society there is also a renewed search to promote apprenticeships as valued ways for people to gain skills and to find enduring and satisfying employment in making things.

We become free to find a better word when we realise that 'disciple' does not occur in the New Testament outside the gospels and Acts. This is because it was a Jewish term and practice and was not known or easily understood in the Greek and Roman world. The New Testament writers were unafraid to replace 'disciple' with other ways to talk about its essence, but in language the hearers could relate to. Two terms – a word and a phrase – are used instead of 'disciple', and both bear upon the issue of what discipleship is for.

The word 'saints' is used of Christians 44 times in the New Testament. Its meaning is that we have been set apart to be God's people – and we are called to be holy like the God we belong to. It is a belonging and becoming word. We are already saints, thanks to the work of Christ, yet we are in the process of becoming more like the title we have been given. Saint is an identity, a direction and a task. We become like the master we are apprenticed to.

There is also the phrase, which appears around 40 times: 'children of God'. Children inherit characteristics from their parents and also learn to copy them. We began as human beings in the image of God, as his creation. But that connection has been spoilt. In Christ this identity is restored. We re-enter his family and are called to that likeness. Ephesians 5:1 picks up this connection: 'Be imitators of God, as beloved children' (ESV). We become like members of the family we belong to.

What is clear is that the issue of becoming Christlike is central. Everyone agrees that *mathetes* is related to learning and that it is one of the core words within the gospel texts. However, what kind of learning and what kind of changes are the questions. I now want to unpack three different kinds of learning that occur and then compare them to the content of the gospels, because they portray relationships between Jesus and the twelve.

Three kinds of learning and Jesus' practice

Professor Ted Ward explains that there are at least three different colours in the rainbow of learning.[6] *Socialisation* learning occurs when children are taught by parental example and command how to hold knife, fork and spoon and what to say at the table. *Formal* learning is happening when a teacher explains when the Battle of Hastings occurred or the usefulness of the mathematical symbol pi. *Non-formal* learning occurs in demonstration and instruction by a craftsman, on how to use a chisel or repair a motor vehicle. Figure 3 shows the pairs which are most traditional, most intentional and inherently practical.

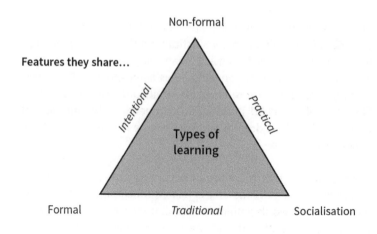

Figure 3: Types of learning

The three can be related. In some cases, all three are going on. For example, newcomers can be socialised into the workplace and take courses, while acquiring shop-floor skills. Thus discipleship could, in theory, be placed at any point within the triangle.

What do we see with the twelve? Mark 3:14 is a suggestive place to start. When Jesus chose them and designated them apostles, his purpose significantly began with these words: 'that they might be *with* him' (my italics). That resonates with the language of socialisation. They gradually get Jesus – his attitudes, values and relationships, as well as his mission and identity – by hanging round him. Later, when they fall out with each other, argue and compete, the correction he gives is mainly remedial socialisation. They are not sent on a formal training course at a discipleship school.

Yet Mark is quite clear that Jesus' purpose is also 'that he might send them', which connects the word apostles and *apostello*, meaning 'to send'. That sending is first embodied in Mark 6:7–13. What they are sent to do is to follow the pattern of what they have seen Jesus do: preach, exorcise and heal. Bear in mind that by this stage their understanding of who he is and what his cross will do would not pass elementary level in theological college. The overall picture at this stage looks most like non-formal learning: gaining tools of the trade by watching the master craftsman and then being told, 'Have a go yourself.' It is about acquiring skills through experience.

There is more than that, and Matthew offers the clue. He goes beyond Mark's version and prepares them to expect suffering. He finishes that section with why they should not fear this: 'It is enough for [apprentices] to be like their teachers' (Matthew 10:25). First-century rabbis accepted disciples so that they would become rabbis. Master craftsmen take apprentices with the same intended trajectory. It is not just acquisition of skills, but also becoming 'like their teacher', like the master. Once more we are in the territory of socialisation as well as non-formal learning.

'Apprentice' suggests that the point is to become like the master craftsman; 'discipleship' must not be content with following behind. Cherry captures the difference: 'Being Christlike... involves following, but that following is not so much trotting along some distance behind Jesus, as about emulating his *way* of travelling.'[7] To highlight his *way* invokes awareness that Christlikeness is about a whole manner of life. It is not so much copying as becoming. This takes us both deeper and higher, developing the 'children of God' image.

Even higher horizons

There is a strand of early church thought called *theosis*. Its astonishing aspiration is found in New Testament texts. Consider them:

> Be perfect... as your heavenly Father is perfect.
> MATTHEW 5:48

> Become mature, attaining to the whole measure of the fullness of Christ.
> EPHESIANS 4:13

Your life is now hidden with Christ in God.
COLOSSIANS 3:3

Through [his promises] you may participate in the divine nature.
2 PETER 1:4

We shall be like him, for we shall see him as he is.
1 JOHN 3:2

The verse from 2 Peter is closest to the meaning of *theosis*. Union with God can only occur when paired with likeness to God. The early church fathers fed on such meat. Read their bold words:

[God] became what we are in order to make us what he is himself.
Irenaeus of Lyons

He who obeys the Lord and follows the prophecy given through him… becomes a god while still moving about in the flesh.
Clement of Alexandria

For the Son of God became man so that men might become gods.
Athanasius

[We] are called 'temples of God' and indeed 'gods', and so we are.
Cyril of Alexandria

Becoming a 'god' is the highest goal of all.
Basil the Great

Become gods for [God's] sake, since [God] became man for our sake.
Gregory of Nazianzus

They were not saying we shall be like God in essence or in his ability to save. But they are saying we are called to become what, in Christ, we already are. Think here of the image of God being restored; imagine entering a fuller unity with God; conceive of having a similarly holy character.

To grow in that sense of identity, purpose and commitment, we will once again meet socialisation and non-formal learning. The place of formal learning is the least significant. Yet are these priorities reflected in how most western Christians see discipleship? I fear not. We need the recovery of the roles of socialisation and non-formal learning in our church communities. We need to see that they are more diagnostic in making disciples than formal learning, especially if it is separated from the other two.

Monks and apprenticeship

New monasticism is one strand of the wide phenomena of fresh expressions of church. It promises to be one of the most significant ones, in that it is designed to bring transformative life, create depth of character forged in the furnace of community life and provide communal, countercultural example.

Monks and friars experienced all the three kinds of learning. However, across the rhythm of their day, and examining their kinds of activity, the vast majority of time and place leans more towards acquiring holy habits by socialisation and non-formal learning. Monks, nuns and friars are formed by participation in the patterns of their community. There is individual prayer and study. That is balanced by serving and work, eating, meeting, deciding and worship, which very much throw them together. These elements of apprenticeship were fortified by the rhythm of the day, the sharing of tasks and the purposes of the varied set of buildings they occupied.

The seven spaces as an apprentice's workshop

I have reread Benedict's prologue with the relationship of the apprentice to the master craftsman in mind. There were many resonances. It begins, 'Listen, my son, to the master's instructions' (P.1). It makes reference to the 'labour of obedience' (P.2) and the 'noble weapons of obedience' (P.30). Work is involved: 'Seeking his workman... the Lord calls him' (P.14). There is an emphasis on good works and good deeds (P.21–22), though knowing it is by God's power (P.29). That work includes growth in character, and so behaviour (P.15–21, 24–28). At the end comes the well-known quote about establishing 'a school for the Lord's service' (P.45), neither harsh nor burdensome, but where needed amending faults and safeguarding love (P.46–47). The monastic life aimed to imbibe spiritual and moral skills and character transformation. The seven spaces testify to the varied aspects of this.

As chapter 3 showed, Cell focuses on inner battles, in the private meeting with God and one's true self. It is the white-hot forge of character and holiness, whose mettle is tested by the other six spaces.

The frequent public element of Chapel, by its rhythms and regularity, teaches discipline in the worship of God. It helps the apprentice resist being driven by emotion or gravitating to self-centred prayer and opens the worshipper to the wide content of scripture.

Chapter is a shop floor to learn about group decision-making. How we communicate, discuss, debate and disagree well is intensely practical. Living wisely with decisions takes time too.

Cloister has unpredictable people traffic. Socialisation is going on all the time in the planned and surprising encounters. It sharpens our ability to live with others and tests our reactions to them.

Garden is clearly a workplace. The skills of tending and nurturing the garden were vital for the community to go on living and not starve.

Fruit or its lack would be obvious. These skills would have to be taught by the experienced to the novices.

Its beneficiary, Refectory, has lessons to teach too. The attitude and practice of serving one another is both socialisation and simple non-formal learning. Learning hospitality, as to Christ, is both good theory and good practice.

The Scriptorium comes closest to domination by formal learning, yet as we saw it was more about learning to pass on knowledge than acquiring it for its own sake. The slow spiritual learning it sought to foster was just as much about how to be transformed into Christlikeness as it was learning healthy theology.

Monastics are apprenticed into the use of all seven spaces. This book has shown both where and how the various Rules name them. More important, it has explored the way the Rules expound the attitudes, virtues and practices needed in the Christian community that uses them. Holy habits are acquired by practice, much of which is communal. Here socialisation and the non-formal are the greater emphasis. These habits then become instincts that fortify the monastery-trained apprentice when the mind wanders, the body protests and the will rebels.

Links to parenting

Suppose you concluded that apprenticeship was a useful way to look at what discipleship means. Maybe your church would explore the seven sacred spaces as shapes and locations to help form a community of apprentices. What might be your role as a leader? Lucy Peppiatt has written about how good discipling can be seen through the lens of what makes for wise parenting in teenage years, with the aim of raising grown-up young adults. I list her bullet points from a ten-page section on parents, apprentices and mission.

Good parents:

- prepare their children to leave home
- adapt to the different phases of a child growing up
- strike a balance between control and freedom
- prepare children to take responsibility, to make good decisions of their own and to form healthy relationships
- give children the freedom to fail
- delight in their children's differences (from themselves and from their siblings)
- impart values by teaching them *and* modeling them
- act as guides and friends throughout a child's life
- depend on their grown up children when they need to exercise humility and model teachability.[8]

'Discipling' in a few Christian circles has an appalling reputation for tight control and spiritual abuse. There is no tinge of that here. Intentional discipleship can coexist with considerable fun. Think of the teasing and safe irreverence that occurs in healthy families with teenagers and young adults. I like Lucy's instincts that balance giving shared values and respecting individuality. I like the trust, mutuality, realism, space and flexible patterns. The traditional gap between cleric and congregation has disappeared here. I close the circle by noting that this good parenting is dominated by socialisation and non-formal learning.

And so it is

I take discipleship to be shorthand for a passionate, obedient following of Jesus because he called me, changed me and as a Christian I now belong to him. The apprentice image emphasises the fact that I follow a master craftsman. By being with him I learn skills and character. The seven spaces are locations within this spiritual communal workshop, each with its specialism. The spaces and discipleship are deeply and usefully connected.

Application questions

- Jot down what you think is the essence of being a Christian.

- Where does your local church put the emphasis around the triangle of three learnings: formal, non-formal or socialisation?

- What evidence is there in your church of the apprentice model at work?

- How many of the seven sacred spaces does your local church community have?

- Describe the parenting style within your congregation/church.

- What effect did the section on *theosis* (pages 171–73) have upon you? Turn your reactions into prayer.

✤ 14 ✤

Stories of journeys through this portal

Northumbria Community

Catherine Askew of Northumbria Community writes…

Our mother house, Nether Springs, reflects our way of life inspired by Celtic monasticism. The site has physical spaces and practices that express the seven sacred spaces, but George's work has made us more conscious of the functions in each space and more aware of holding the seven spaces for community in 'monastery on the road' gatherings outside Nether Springs.

Our two strongest spaces are consistently Chapel and Refectory. Corporate prayer from *Celtic Daily Prayer* and eating together seem to happen anywhere and anytime we meet!

Cell is a huge emphasis, and we encourage each other to regularly enter what is often the scariest and most transforming of spaces. At Nether Springs, we do have spaces set aside, *poustinias*, with hope of more to come. When people come out of the cell, they often look different. I imagine they have been stoking the fire in their hearts, and, although the door to the stove is closed, the light and warmth radiate out anyway.

Scriptorium is the space we are probably putting the most emphasis on at the moment. We have many treasures as a community, but many of them have been tucked away and some even forgotten. We are consciously returning to our foundations to seek again these treasures and gather around them to learn through the school for monastic living. One woman who is sensitive to the history of places sensed that the library at Nether Springs used to be a smithy. She wondered if the nice cosy fire is in the sitting room, but the really hot fire, which can change things, is actually in the Scriptorium space. We're still pondering this insight.

Every Monday morning at Nether Springs we have our Chapter meeting. This takes place in our dining room, combining Refectory and Chapter, and thus tea/toast and decision-making. This is a significant time to work out the practicalities of the week ahead, but also a reflective, learning space as we celebrate where we have seen God at work, witness to personal joys or struggles and offer suggestions on where we need to tweak our shared life or revisit why we do what we do. If someone is on the team for just a week or two, they too come to the Chapter meeting, and often the questions and observations from the newest team members are the most revealing. As a worldwide community, we are too many and scattered to have a consensus model for decision-making, but we are seeking ways to listen more deeply to one another, so that decisions are made with more perspectives in the Chapter room than those who are physically present. In the past years, we haven't been as intentional as we might have been to hear all the voices that need to be heard.

For me, Cloister has turned into a practice since engaging with the seven spaces. My days are often very planned, but Cloister is the space in particular where God might bring me into an encounter with someone I've been cleverly avoiding or into a conversation I don't think I have time for, but it's all in God's time. It's a place of getting from A to B; but more significantly, it is a place of holy interruption as you meet with others 'on the way'.

Garden is a place of the miracle of life. To work outdoors with purpose is surely one of the most refreshing activities in which we can engage. I've seen a team member in absolute wonderment at the growth of a cucumber, another drinking in the satisfaction of having completed the rabbit-proof fence and two coming back from the garden with full containers and an easy gait, having harvested berries together. Yet it's the place where there is perennially more to do than we have time for, so it's hard not to feel behind or beholden to the garden. As we are especially inspired by Celtic monasticism, our community gatherings in different locations often have an emphasis on time in creation and, if the weather isn't cooperating, time spent creating alone and together can have a similar effect.

While it's the way these spaces work together that brings wholeness, I think different seasons allow for emphases on certain spaces, and that is entirely appropriate for growth.

The Barn, Bardney, Lincolnshire

Pete Atkins relates seven sacred spaces and The Barn…

My wife and I bought a derelict Grade-2 listed barn in October 2010. Our understanding of the vision for it at that stage was:

- it would be our home and a place to gather our family
- it would be a place for gathering and supporting pioneers
- it would be a prayer house and base for a local mission team.

As we prayed and considered how to design the barn before applying for planning permission and listed-building consent, we were significantly influenced by our understanding of Celtic monasticism, 24/7 movement boiler rooms and not least by thinking around the seven sacred spaces.

There were several empty houses around the barn, and we wondered if it would become the centre of a multi-dwelling, intentional community. This in particular led us to consider carefully the wisdom of the seven sacred spaces as we envisioned the spaces we would create and adapt architecturally in The Barn.

We were significantly influenced by what we understood of Celtic monasticism – reinforced by the fact that King Oswald of Northumbria was buried in Bardney for 200 years. His relics were the endowment (c. 675) and the focus of pilgrimage to the middle Saxon Abbey – described by Bede as 'the great Abbey at Bardney'. There was also a Benedictine abbey in Bardney from 1086 to 1539. The seven sacred spaces approach would accurately reflect its life and architecture. We gradually understood that God was calling us to be a prayer-based community learning from the wisdom of others who have lived life in this way, reflected in their built spaces.

We became increasingly convinced of the need to completely reimagine church in the rural areas of the UK. The full description in seven sacred spaces of what life in community as Christians (aka church) can be like inspired us, as we developed a mixed economy of church in the village. We understood that life together as Christians was intended to be far more than just a weekly chapel gathering and that all the seven spaces together, and the activity they reflect, form authentic church. What has developed over subsequent years is a prayer-based, mission-focused community, which now has six households involved and is integrated well with the existing churches in the village.

The seven sacred spaces approach has acted as a guide and source of affirmation for the way our community does life together:

- **Cell**: Each household has its own bedrooms or cell spaces for sleep, prayer and study. In addition we have a number of extra bedrooms in The Barn and other homes that act as cell for those visiting or resident. We also have a *poustinia* for retreat in that way.

- **Chapel**: We have a prayer room which we made usable before any other space in the house. We have established a flexible rhythm of prayer and worship in different-sized groups: daily, weekly and monthly with ad hoc additions. We have developed a Bardney prayer for common and corporate use.

- **Chapter**: We meet to plan and take community decisions weekly – usually in the prayer room and in the context of prayer and worship. We also have a monthly gathering in the prayer room and kitchen – 'Revs' breakfast', when the church leaders of all denominations in the village meet for prayer, breakfast and planning.

- **Cloister**: Our cloisters are the paths around the garden and ample circulation space indoors, our upstairs landing and the open-plan downstairs area.

- **Garden**: We grow some of our own fruit and vegetables but have also created the garden as a place of play and fun for children, recreation for adults and prayer and contemplation for all.

- **Refectory**: We have a big kitchen and refectory tables. We can seat more than 20 people and often do when we have our monthly 'Communi-tea'. The kitchen is also one source of home baking for the coffee shop we run in the village. We express our values as Candle (the presence of God), Table (community, family and learning) and Door (welcoming in and sending out in mission).

- **Scriptorium**: We have creative retreat days and musicians staying and writing, and we have children's and adults' book clubs, though these meet in another refectory – our village Christian coffee shop. We also have plans for the conversion of stable units into a creative space/art studio. Writing also happens in many of our spaces, including a study.

DNA Networks, Colchester

David Beales describes the spaces as a framework for a multiple ministries centre...

Colchester's DNA Networks became a Bishops' Mission Order of the Anglican Diocese of Chelmsford in 2013. The bishop of Chelmsford licensed me as pioneer minister of DNA Networks until early 2018. I then moved to a different role, overseeing a range of pioneering projects and church plants in the area. I remain in touch with DNA Networks, but no longer have formal responsibilities there.

Our philosophy of ministry had centred on releasing the godly dreams that emerged in the people who prayed and worshipped with us. We didn't start with a neat or clear strategy, except that we wanted to see what God was up to in different people groups around the town. The result was that we had piloted a number of mission units, led by micro-communities of two or three people. Some of these emerged into S-LIM churches – Spirit-Led, Incarnational, Multiplying.

We had occupied a two-storey building for five years, during which some of the mission units and S-LIM churches had emerged. It included a large, warm space downstairs and a smaller upstairs hall and kitchen, together with four offices. The lease on our building expired in 2017, so we needed new premises in which to operate this variety of ministries. The diocese offered us the former St James' Rectory, at 76 East Hill in Colchester, after the previous incumbent had retired. In April 2017 we needed to make space for the following ministries:

- refugee integration, both face-to-face encounters and backroom office support
- children's ministry, parent and toddler groups
- Christians Against Poverty groups
- adult and family worship

- footballers' breakfasts
- community lunches and assorted celebrations
- discussions and meetings to plan and organise
- office space for administering the activities of the mission units and S-LIM churches.

How were we going to fit everything in? The seven sacred spaces provided a model for fitting all the different mission units into the space offered by the building. I outlined to my efficient and pragmatic colleague Mark Snelling what the seven sacred spaces were about, stressing the way our values could be evenly represented, so as to avoid competition between the various ministries. There was nothing slavish about the allocation of space. We were not going to prohibit eating food in the chapel or having meetings in the garden. The seven sacred spaces were rather a means of protecting values and priorities, so that one concern did not get overrun by another.

Chapel was expressed in the former living room. Chairs were placed around the wall so that up to 24 people could be fairly comfortably accommodated in a square-shaped room, creating the possibility for a warm, participatory and interactive worship environment.

An upstairs room was dedicated to children's worship, although much of this activity moved outside during the summer. This was somewhat like Scriptorium, since the scriptures were told, painted, drawn, coloured-in and acted out, and creativity was encouraged. Certainly, this space became the focus for passing on faith to children, as well as praying and singing with them.

The former dining room became Chapter. Most meetings of up to ten people could take place there. However, this also became the room in which morning prayer was held with anything from two to six people. It has also been the overflow room from Chapel, complete with TV monitor, when more than 24 people have gathered for worship or when parents wanted to nurse infants but still hear what was going on.

The kitchen became Refectory, where light refreshments could be served to small groups or where a few people could gather to share a cup of coffee. However, with larger groups, the Refectory function spread into the Garden, the Chapter house and the Chapel.

The sizeable physical garden was originally less a place of work as a place for recreation, children's play, sharing food and communal worship during summer months. However, the considerable workforce needed office workspace. Three rooms upstairs became administrative offices for church matters, the refugee project and finance; this was their field of work. Downstairs, the former rector's study became an office with desks, phones and printers, where client consultations could take place with people using the refugee service.

Upstairs, the smallest bedroom was dedicated as a Cell. This was allocated for personal prayer or small prayerful encounters with up to three people.

The corridor downstairs was lined with chairs, so that people could chat with one another while waiting for a consultation. This was deliberately set up to be like the Cloister, but, in truth, the whole downstairs area and the garden became the place for planned or spontaneous encounters.

By April 2019, some of the ministries had dispersed or stopped; other projects have emerged in response to needs and issues. However, the seven distinct spaces continue, although the current teams would struggle to name them by these labels. The centre has remained a place for daily prayer, taking time to hear and discuss the scriptures and to bring before God the needs and concerns of the day.

We may not have made absolutely the best use of the space, but we certainly preserved the values that were important to us; so the seven sacred spaces model remains a useful tool for planning the overlapping aspects of varied ongoing work.

St Thomas' Community, Derby

Simon Cartwright tells of the birth of St Thomas' Community...

It's a busy inner-city street in Derby. You pass numerous take-aways, phone shops and food stores offering cuisines from all over the globe. Running off to left and right are narrow terraced streets, largely occupied by migrant groups who first settled in the area before they raised enough money to move out. Opposite the library and police station and next to the health centre lies St Thomas. This is a decaying Victorian church. In 2011, a tree was growing out of the roof and rain was pouring in. The congregation struggled due to old age and ill health, so it was decided to close the church and merge the congregation with the neighbouring parish.

I was appointed as community minister to reimagine the role of the church and re-engage with the community. However, deciding to close the St Thomas building felt like putting a sign on the door saying 'the church has given up on you'.

So I began a twin approach: building partnerships around community development projects and exploring whether God was calling us to replant the church. Working alongside FareShare, the church was opened up once a fortnight to receive waste food from the food industry to pass on to food distribution projects in Derby. At the same time a small group began to gather at St Thomas for a weekly prayer meeting. It was a small beginning for a big vision to reopen St Thomas.

Fast-forward to 2016 and resurrection was beginning. The small prayer group had grown to about twelve people and become a missional community – committed to prayer, hospitality and engaging in mission with the community.

Over half a million pounds was raised to repair and renovate the church – the building is now watertight and structurally sound, with a new kitchen, toilets and heating. Additional funds would create breakout spaces for community projects and an office for social enterprises.

There were some questions. Were we merely creating a community centre or reopening the church as it was? Neither was satisfactory. We wanted to look at a new model of church, so paradoxically we turned to ancient paths. We looked at monasticism, when churches were open 24/7. They offered worship but also a school, hospital and guest house. We did not see St Thomas as a retreat house but rather as a busy place combining conversation, prayer and refreshment. But we were also aware that underpinning these monasteries was a religious community dedicated to prayer, hospitality and mission.

As the people at St Thomas' Community began to journey together, we found we began to develop a shared purpose. We had many gifts, skills and talents and began to sense a vocation to help develop this project. At the same time, we noticed that people were searching for a deeper level of commitment, both to the group relationally and to the mission. We began to find that new monasticism helped us explore the outworking of the kingdom of God for individuals, Christian communities and society at large.

Three distinct themes began to emerge:

- a call to pray for one another, for the church community and for those in the area
- a call to work on the margins – we are on a mission to those on the edge
- a call to hospitality – a shared meal is at the heart of our worship, while giving food is key to our outreach.

These three themes began to coalesce around a rhythm of life. These owned themes encouraged a pattern for our community as a rhythm of living. This was not a mission statement, setting aims and objectives. Rather we were asking a more fundamental question –

how should we live out the gospel in this context? It was about making explicit what is implicit about the way the community was formed. This not only helped us understand who we are, but it also enabled those not part of the St Thomas' Community to understand our values and the type of church we sought to be.

It was intriguing how St Thomas' Community began to shape its rhythm of life and the way the creation of new physical spaces in the building echoed the development of our spiritual life, both as individuals and as a community. In connecting to the building project, we began to identify eight sacred spaces of a monastery in our building plans.

At the same time, the group began to explore being part of the Society of the Holy Trinity – a network of new monastic communities living in urban contexts. To help these separate communities form their rhythm of life, we were asked eight core questions that would be answered in different ways according to context.

What was an interesting – dare I say godly – coincidence is how these eight questions directly related not only to our community life but also to the physical spaces in our building and how they contributed to shaping each member's own spiritual life.

- **Cell/prayer** – *a space to be alone with God*: How can we grow in prayer individually and in community, listening and in stillness, daily and within a weekly rhythm?
- **Chapel/worship** – *a space for devotion/prayer with others*: How can we grow in leading and participating in communal worship and in the giving of time and resources?
- **Library/study** – *a space of learning to grow in knowledge*: How can we develop biblical and personal reflection, reading and study?
- **Chapter/meeting** – *a space for discussion and exchanging views*: How can we model community life through reconciliation; listening to God and to others; choosing to forgive; sharing hope and love; and humility and peace-making?

- **Refectory/sharing meals** – *a space for eating together*: How can we practise hospitality by welcoming the stranger, the isolated and the lonely and by preparing and sharing food?
- **Cloister/mission** – *a space connecting church and the world*: How do we respond in compassionate action to the needs of our neighbours, the voiceless, the poor and the excluded?
- **Garden/work** – *a space of labour and productivity*: How do we follow Christ in our work, serving God through our labour and integrating values of our faith in our places of work?
- **Infirmary/well-being** – *a space for healthy work and rest*: How do we receive the love of God by balancing work, rest and play, by pursuing activities that give life and by seeking the good, the true and the beautiful in all and for all?

The sacred spaces project identified spaces in an historic monastery and showed how these resonated with spiritual spaces in church life today. In St Thomas' Community, we found that the physical space and discipleship spaces overlapped.

So it is about sacred spaces in a building but also about sacred spaces in time. We needed space allocated in time for these different aspects of prayer, mission and hospitality. It had to impact our building plans, community life and individual walk with God.

We have not completed our journey – the building work is not complete and the community is still in its infancy – but reflection on sacred spaces has been an important part of our discernment process. We wait to see how we get on building a 21st-century monastery in a 19th-century church in the middle of the inner city.

Harlequin Arts

Karen Herrick relates the seven spaces to her ministry through Harlequin Arts…

The striking illustration of the seven spaces wheel in harmony (see page 148) is in marked contrast to seeing them distorted (see page 149). In speaking, George Lings uses an exercise by which listeners assess which of their seven spaces are more developed and which are underdeveloped. [This is shown in the application section at the end of chapter 10.] This visual growing into the seven sacred spaces enables many to access its holistic teaching. It gives a variety of intellectual and spiritual levels that would not appeal in the same way if conveyed in a purely written form. Certainly, for myself and those I have encountered, who find depth in a creative spirituality, this has been the case.

I was first introduced to the concept of seven sacred spaces while on a mission and ministry course in 2016. The creative, colourful image of growing into the seven spaces really struck a chord, initially enabling me to focus on gaining a deeper understanding of my own spiritual life in a holistic way, and then going on to incorporate its wisdom into both my own artwork and creative quiet days that I lead.

At the time of my introduction to seven sacred spaces, I had been, at the beginning of each year, taking a key word that was relevant to my life, to explore as part of my own spiritual discipline, focusing on all that God might have to say to me through the lens of that word. In 2015, my word had been 'journey' and, for the first time as an artist, I had decided to record my thought processes not only in journal form but also visually in stitch, creating artwork each month that documented my spiritual journey, while sharing both the image and the words online via a blog (**harlequinarts.co.uk/index.php/blog/sanctuary-in-stitch**). After twelve months of a deeper prayer life and increased understanding of ways in which I felt God was leading me, I decided to continue the practice of creating stitched artworks containing biblical narratives and themes, creatively journaling my spiritual journey as I travelled.

When I came across the seven sacred spaces, my word for the year was 'dwell', and I had been seeking a better way of dwelling in God, a more harmonious way of living than the discord of an imbalanced, over-busy lifestyle. So it was that the seven sacred spaces spoke into my life and allowed artwork to be created, as a personal response, to form part of my 'dwell' series. I stitched the wheel deliberately off-centre (as shown on the front cover), to express my own imbalance, encourage others to contemplate where they might position their own centre and how central God might be in their own lives and perhaps also encourage others to dwell on key spaces that might need attention and tuning.

When exhibited, the artworks I create act as visual narratives that enable conversations about our individual and corporate faith journey. I use them in experiential creative retreats and quiet days that I run, encouraging others to pray creatively through stitch, collage, weaving or other mediums.

Through the springboard of the illustration, *Dwelling in the Seven Sacred Spaces*, and the subsequent artwork, retreatants have prayerfully and creatively explored ways in which we might nurture a balanced lifestyle, providing rhythm to our Christian lives, focusing on drawing closer to God through a variety of creative mediums, allowing the colour, shape and textures of the materials we choose to enable God to speak into our lives.

I was often asked if I had cards with the images that had been helpful to participants during their retreat, so I began to print cards with words on the reverse to facilitate faith conversations and hopefully deepen the faith of others. Both the simplicity and colour of the illustration, I think, are key to the power of its visual narrative. And it is that which seems to draw the creative deeper into the wisdom of the seven sacred spaces.

A Benedictine tertiary

Sue Hope, a tertiary of an Anglican sisterhood of nuns aligned with the Rule of Benedict, writes...

It is frequently the case that if you join an organisation you find among the resultant paperwork a small card to put in your wallet, usually bearing an outline of the values or advantages of belonging. I find that the seven sacred spaces approach acts in the same way for me. It outlines the values of the order to which I belong and acts as a kind of shorthand. I hold it in my mind and heart not as a list but as an ikon – an image of the monastic buildings which informs me and reminds me of the values which I am trying to live. Like carrying around the photograph of a beloved person or place, I can metaphorically take it out of my pocket, look at it and immediately be reminded of who I am and what I am for and about. So, for example, I can see the stability of the monastic buildings and the commitment to 'place', an expression of the incarnate Christ who located himself in a particular time and place in our world, and thus has made himself locatable in *all* times and places. Or I can see the places set apart for prayer, for work, for food and for fellowship – and the spaces through which the community must move from one to another – and am reminded of the constant need for balance in daily life.

But isn't an ikon of buildings a bit static? How can this kind of ikon, which stands for 'institutional life', resonate with our free-flowing, postmodern culture, with its suspicion of heavy buildings, of ordered regularity, of 'rules' applied to life? But just as an ikon only fulfils its true purpose when the eyes which gaze at it succeed in passing through the picture to the reality beyond, so a contemplative gaze at the monastic buildings may reveal other pictures emerging. Three things particularly strike me in my contemplation of the seven sacred spaces in relation to our postmodern culture: reflexivity, creativity and liminality.

The invitation to reflexivity

Sociologists James Holstein and Jaber Gubrium draw attention to the work of psychologist Kenneth J. Gergen, who has written extensively on the overloading of 'the self' in western culture: 'The postmodern world is so full of meanings that it risks saturating the self. Filled to overflowing, the self loses any distinct identity.'[1] Interpreting Gergen, they continue:

> While there is no doubt that such a self 'knows itself' from social experience, ironically, it is most likely to really 'find itself' *away* from the social. In seclusion, it can take stock of who it is and what life is all about… It requires a measure of separation from others, distance from the world, in order to function properly. In a word, it needs to be periodically 're-centred' to be experientially secured.[2]

Cell, in particular, invites me to take seriously the need for space to think, to reflect theologically, to refind myself in God. Cell is not a flight from the world; it is an opportunity for theological reflection upon myself as I engage with the world, reassessing, re-evaluating, repositioning, in light of the gospel and the love of God. It goes without saying that the invitation to reflexivity may require the self-discipline of withdrawal from social media and from the competing voices of other selves that clamour for me to live by them and not by 'every word which proceeds from the mouth of God'.

The invitation to creativity

Recently I have been enjoying drawing and painting, working in a variety of media, and I have been reminded again of how creativity goes hand-in-hand with 'hard work'. It is hard work to try again and again to draw the same figure, an arm, a face, a flower, a pot, a bottle or a row of rooftops. Application, perspiration and intentionality are all part of creativity. In the ikon of the monastic buildings, the garden is the place both of hard work and of creativity. Hedges are bent and braided into windbreaks. Potato beds are dug, trees are espaliered, peaches are grown carefully and lovingly in the greenhouses. Beehives need checking, cleaning and restoring. Blight must be resisted, and wildlife must be managed. The effort results in something beautiful. Fruitfulness and loveliness emerge together, one of a piece. Our hard work is creative, and our creativity is hard work.

This creativity is not limited to the type of work which produces things that we can see. There is creative work too in the infirmary, the kitchens and the administrative block. Shared laughter at the bedside of an end-of-life patient can be creative. Life is made 'wholly holy' by the presence of God's indwelling Spirit: it becomes creative, many-coloured, multifaceted – a tapestry in which, in particular, the dark strands give depth and form.

The invitation to liminality

If the monastic buildings appear static, the movement through them is anything but. We know the cloister connects. It links up the other places; people walk up and down them. They use this space to change gear. It is a place of surprising encounters; we may meet the person we are trying to avoid but to bump into a beloved friend will be a joy. For me, the ikon of the cloister signals liminality. Liminal space is 'threshold space'; it is space between worlds. We inhabit it in between other things, events and life moments, on our way from somewhere to somewhere. It's the space I inhabit when I am uncertain about 'What next? Where next?' It signposts the importance and the vitality of transitional moments in our lives. Living on the threshold, with uncertainty, with paradox, with puzzles and with questions, is an exhilarating, unnerving place to be. Hanging between earth and heaven, the cross of Christ is *the* great image of liminality.

On a more humdrum level, I find the ikon of the cloister, with its free-flowing movements, its openness to whoever I might meet, its endless possibilities of conversation, of newness, invites me to live peacefully with contingency and uncertainty, not seeking to manipulate future events for my own ends but rather allowing things to come to me. Liminality invites me to let go.

Llandaff Diocese

Richard Lowndes explains the influence of the seven sacred spaces in Llandaff Diocese…

A diocesan colleague, Val Hamer, read about the seven sacred spaces in an 'Encounters on the Edge' booklet. For her, it was not an experience 'on the edge' but central, full of potential and full of health – like your five-a-day! We set out with this idea to develop a tool which would be a means of fresh expression for our diocese. We would look through the lens of these spaces and see what emerged for each context.

Ultimately, the tool was project-managed into existence using video clips of examples and using the spaces at three levels: we invited people to look at what the spaces meant to them individually, what they meant to the gathered church community and, most importantly, what they meant in the wider community. We grounded each space in Bible study and provided additional liturgical and prayer resources to embed this in our faith.

We piloted the tool in several places before it reached its final form. The parish context was important, but we also used it with children and, most interestingly, in a prison. The prisoners got the concept immediately, despite our being anxious about explaining Cell as a place of prayer! It produced writing and reflection that gave huge learning to all those involved.

An early issue was one of accessibility. How accessible are words like Cloister and Scriptorium to people inside the church, let alone the general public? The word 'Scriptorium' was changed to 'Library' and we then set about developing 'shadow' words for all the spaces, so that people could quickly access what we might be getting at:

Cell	*pray*
Chapel	*worship*
Chapter	*decide*
Cloister	*meet*
Garden	*work*
Refectory	*share*
Library	*study*

Using all this thinking we decided to launch a booklet with a DVD for use across the diocese in 2013, under the title *Rediscovering and Revealing God's Kingdom through Seven Sacred Spaces*.

'Do not launch this in a religious building' was the cry in my head, so we began looking for a venue in Cardiff which would fit for us, such as the rugby stadium or a big hotel (both costly). Finally, we had an offer from a member of the Welsh Parliament to hold it in the Senedd (government) building in Cardiff free of charge! This is a building surrounded by glass, in which we were able to demonstrate all seven spaces easily: a seat of decision-making where we could demonstrate hospitality, encounter each other, pray together or apart, study together and go about embedding our endeavour, as a church relevant to all.

The development of a DVD demonstrating good examples of the practice across the diocese meant that for the first time we were encouraging each other to not keep these things to ourselves, but to shout it from the rooftops, though by nature of a fixed format these examples became out of date quite quickly.

How do you use an approach like this strategically? This was the question to grapple with. Mainly we used it where there was energy for engagement rather than forcing it. There was a year when we used it for the archdeacons' annual reports on parish activity and statistics. There was no energy for that. However, when parishes wanted to do some vision-setting or when there was a need for funding for mission initiatives, there was much more creative engagement. The real beauty of the seven spaces came to the fore when it was not used as a stick to beat people with, but when they could engage and see for themselves that, actually, they occupied every space in one form or another; then they were able to see God's invitation to grow more fully into that space.

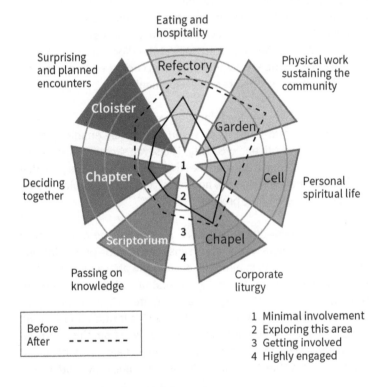

Figure 4: Assessing growth into each space

After discerning the areas in which God is calling you to grow, it becomes possible to form an action plan. The action plan we developed was intentionally credal as a statement of belief in what we are called by God to fulfil in each space. We never dictated how these should be used; for some it was a short-term project plan, while for others it formed part of an ongoing, renewable action plan in a five-year cycle.

Being called to grow into these spaces led us to think about those involved in our discernment process for ordination and reader training. We developed a new questionnaire based on the seven spaces and used the measuring tool at the diocesan discernment panel to assess how fully individuals occupied each space and therefore where their points for development were.

As a diocese we are also forming ministry areas – areas of collaboration and sharing of resources which enable greater engagement, growth and creativity. The seven sacred spaces were a great way for identifying to parishes their potential and the potential of their partners in ministry, and often a joint action plan would emerge at the end of the process.

At this point in our diocese we were in a time of enormous change and transition; there was no clear sense of everyone promoting one vision for the future so, although each of the above initiatives had some strategic intent, there was no real push from the centre to promote this tool as the way forward to unite us in a common goal. Doubtless some would have railed against it if that had been the case. Ultimately there was a need to move away from this approach to usher in a new era. The benefits of the project are still evident, and it still has life within it, as some still use it. It comes alive with use.

Requests have come from parishes in Wales and England to use it, and currently it is being made available, via the diocese and our All-Wales Theological Education Institution, St Padarn's, to the whole of Wales, as part of a package of resources called 'Living and Learning'.

The theme of working together and partnership has been strong in the use of this tool. Our link diocese of Uppsala, Sweden, has worked with us and translated some of the resources into Swedish. They too have used it across their diocese but also in the Swedish Church overseas. It was a great joy to be the keynote speaker at a conference in Uppsala and find that there was to be a presentation from the Swedish Church in Melbourne on their use of the seven sacred spaces.

The initial feeling of my colleague, that this was a health check for our life of faith, has proved fruitful to us (like those five-a-day). We stand humbled and grateful to George Lings for spotting these spaces and writing about them so that we too might rediscover and reveal God's kingdom.

Messy Church

Lucy Moore connects Messy Church and the seven spaces…

I once spent a happy afternoon dreaming up an architect's plan of the perfect building in which to hold a Messy Church. This circular building, surrounded by enclosed but wild gardens, centred round a palatial kitchen that opened on to nearly every room, so the all-important cooks' team could be involved throughout, and continuous refreshment could be poured out of the kitchen into the welcome room, the activity room and the meal room. These rooms, designed in décor and furniture for the comfort of people of all ages, correlated with many of the seven sacred spaces: a Cloister space just inside the front door for welcoming people as they arrive and bumping into them for serendipitous conversation afterwards; a literal Garden combined with Scriptorium – an outdoor and indoor space for combining learning and play with the physicality of connection with the earth; a Chapel for the gathered celebration and, of course, a Refectory for that all-important meal. It was a beautiful dream, although it will never be built anywhere but at the top of my ivory tower.

The learning point from the seven sacred spaces concept for Messy Churches as we develop and mature is perhaps how to engage with two spaces that are less obviously already part of the structure of a normal Messy Church. Chapter and Cell spaces are nowhere to be found in my blueprint. Adding yet another room on to an already labyrinthine building complex wouldn't be required for Chapter or Cell, as all Messy Church teams are adept at adapting and making do. Let Chapter meet in the Refectory! Let Cell happen in the Garden! But the reminder that these need to happen somehow is timely.

How are decisions made in Messy Church? The planning already tends to be done by a team rather than one individual, so perhaps the Chapter is Gloria's sofa or Steve's dining room table. My colleague Dave Martin, when working full-time for an Anglican church, instituted a 'Messy CC' to complement the PCC – a decision-making group comprised of team members and interested family members to shape the Messy Church. It was part of its ongoing discipleship. This asked for more contribution from different people, so they became more contributors and less consumers, leading to greater belonging while still being accountable to the wider local church.

Other Messy Churches have so many team members now that the leadership team of the church (PCC, eldership, vestry or similar) might well be largely made up of people involved in both inherited and Messy forms of worship. With the norm of Messy leaders being already overstretched and finding it hard to fit in anything extra, perhaps making a Chapter space within the actual Messy Church itself is more helpful, including a regular activity that invites people young and old to share their ideas and opinions through creative approaches, like adding smiley and frowny faces to a board or popping beans into containers to represent their opinion.

Cell is a challenge for Messy Churches, where so much is deliberately communal and corporate; we tend to talk about 'families' rather than 'individuals', for example, as so many people come as a family group of whatever make-up that might be. While families are important, as we learn from and with each other, is enough priority given to personal response to the challenges of discipleship? Part of a current project on discipleship involves making sure each individual, young or old, who wants one has a way of recording their spiritual journey over the period the project is running. BRF publishes a range of resources to help the spirituality of Messy leaders, team members and family members, encouraging everyone to explore the Bible, prayer and worship. We could do more to encourage people to encounter God at school, home and work, and the Church of England's 'Setting God's People Free' movement provides help for this.

Is there any insight that Messy Church might offer to the seven sacred spaces? Perhaps it's worth considering the Messy Church emphasis on the Kitchen rather than the Refectory. In both, hospitality and the provision of food is key. A Refectory is somewhere to consume the food, while a Kitchen is for the communal loving and imaginative preparation of that food. A Refectory places value on the eaters; a Kitchen places value on the cooks and washer-uppers. One of the problems of inherited church is that it seems to be perfectly acceptable to say, 'I come to church to be fed,' rather than 'I am part of a church that feeds Christ's sheep.' Valuing the Kitchen is something to do with being the priesthood of all believers rather than the passive recipients of priestly benefaction. Perhaps if the tough creative worship offered in the Kitchen was valued by being named as a sacred space, rather than simply the consumption of that food around the table in the Refectory, it could help change the attitude of some church members into a more generous, responsible and sacrificial one that puts the worship needs of those who aren't yet members before one's own personal preferences.

Another potential learning point from comparing the seven sacred spaces with Messy Church is the blithe assumption I made in my architectural dreams that while it would be apt for the Kitchen to have serving hatches into the Cloister, Scriptorium/Garden and Refectory, it would not be appropriate or necessary to have a similar hatch into the Chapel. But what insights might be gained by linking the Chapel, too, with the Kitchen? At a simple level, we would be making it possible for the cooks' team to join in every aspect of Messy Church, even as they prepare the food. Nobody is excluded. No one can hide either from the whole family of God or from another space in which to encounter God. The Kitchen's everyday practicality becomes linked to the words, music, silence and sanctity of the Chapel. The Chapel's worship is linked to the material food and drink that comes from the Kitchen: the bread, 'work of human hands' and the 'fruit of the vine' are then part of the hallowed nature of the everyday.

Chapel can be found at every home's kitchen table; the divide between sacred and secular is broken down. And if we're getting serious about the sacred and the spiritual, we could talk for a long time about the importance of a decent Lavatorium. But alas, space, sacred or otherwise, does not permit.

The range of stories widens

I continue to hear further stories of people entering the seven sacred spaces portal. It has been employed as the Lent course in a parish in Gloucester diocese, and it shapes One Life, that diocese's sports ministry. A teacher of the mission-shaped ministry course uses it to explore the topic 'What is church?' It is one lens for self-understanding within Urban Abbey, a prayer-focused inner-urban intentional community in Nottingham, and it has been one element in training readers in Leicester diocese. It was used quite subconsciously to reorder a redundant inner-city church in Belfast, starting with Refectory and only much later in the process adding the function of Chapel. I wonder what other unknown stories are out there.

✣ 15 ✣

Making your own journey

What the seven spaces will not do

They are *not* a quick fix

The seven sacred spaces assist a person learning how to be alone and also together. Neither journey is quick or easy, or without ups and downs. To adopt them as a continuing way to look at life invites a lifetime of change. When used by a person, church or diocese, they must be viewed as the task of a decade, not the content of a short course. You can no more acquire the practice of spiritual disciplines by attending a tea party in a monastery.

The seven spaces do not work automatically, all by themselves; rather, they are places that enable characteristic kinds of spiritual and social encounter. Think of them as a 'way in' sign. In addition, because they are always occupied by fallen people and deal with spiritual issues, they are open to misuse and can be linked to particular temptations.

With some groups I have set an exercise to consider each space in relation to the classic vices, using the eastern list of Cassian's eight afflictions that need guarding against. To balance that, I asked them which virtues will be especially needed in each place. All the groups found it was not true that each space has only one vice to be aware of and one virtue to foster. That fits with Benedict's teaching. His Rule focuses on the virtue of humility that applies widely across them. Benedictine Meg Funk claims that humility is to be seen as the classic Christian virtue, when compared with those characteristic of other religions.[1]

All this underlines that more is needed than the spaces themselves. They do not in themselves provide the transformation of life into Christlikeness that we seek. Reflect on another word we use about spaces – 'facilities'. The seven spaces facilitate spiritual transformation; they aid or assist it, but they do not magically provide it. The fundamental need is of grace that comes through living encounter with Jesus Christ. That is assisted by another grace, to be shaped by glad acceptance of the message of scripture. It is no accident that the Rule of Benedict and the Celtic Rules are littered with quotes from scripture. Then, both following Christ and being under scripture are translated into life, in the surprising and unpredictable power of the Holy Spirit released within us. Whether that happens very slowly, which is more common, or in visible sudden steps, it is a lifelong journey. That process has a glorious destiny, known in the Greek fathers tradition as *theosis* – or becoming godlike, which chapter 12 explained.

I am entertained by the word 'habits'. It refers to the clothing worn by monks and to repeated practices that become habitual. There is a proverb: sow a thought and reap an action; sow an action and reap a habit; sow a habit and reap a destiny. I have also heard that only an action done 20 times is likely to become a habit. There is nothing quick going on here, but good habits will fortify us when the spirit is faint, the body rebels and the mind is in turmoil.

They are *not* a strategy

The seven spaces are vocational locations, and therefore they cannot be imposed without losing the life that can only come through their voluntary and eventually covenanted adoption. This shift beyond being just voluntary reflects the overall monastic process which begins with enquiry. Enquiry is followed by a novitiate, or learning to live the values, itself tested by the discernment of others.

Concluded, it leads to the taking of vows – making a covenant with God. Something similar occurred in the early church. Initial enquiry was followed by a few years of being in the *catechumenate* – learning the faith and its disciplines. When completed, baptism on Easter Day followed – another covenant with God. For this reason, the seven spaces approach cannot be a structural fix for the ills of an individual group, church or diocese.

They *cannot* be made to 'work' everywhere untranslated

Local church experience has shown that the language around the seven spaces can need translation in context. This is not just because some unfamiliar words, like Scriptorium, are polysyllabic. It is also because some words have different meanings in varied contexts. Cell means different things to monks, prisoners and biologists. This need to translate should not surprise us. The incarnation reveals a process of willing change to engage with context, while remaining faithful to an unchanging essential. There is consistency in that God the Son came to earth, while there was change in that Jesus of Nazareth, son of Mary, came to exist.

The seven labels are not sacrosanct. However, it is then all the more important to understand the values beneath each one. Without this, the process of necessary translation could be corrupted. There is evidence in the wider church, over recent decades, of a worrying tendency to uncritically copy something that appears to 'work' elsewhere. This may be born out of anxiety to do something or the tendency to follow a brand. It might come from an illusion that you can ignore context, or it might just be lazy pragmatism.

This pattern of copying has damaged the spread of cell-church thinking, the true adoption of Messy Church and the misunderstanding of general principles that apply to fresh expressions of church. In all cases the tendency has been to copy the shapes of a meeting, but to fail to understand the values that led to the adoption of a particular shape in the original context.[2] In my judgement, this disastrous resultant downgrading has neither called into question the validity of the original, nor has the fault been with the originators. Moreover, good ways forward have been hampered and stilted. As a result, unreflective local leaders say, 'We tried it and it didn't work,' whereas the reality was that it was not properly tried. Identifying core values within each space is very important, otherwise there is a real danger that the language will be adopted, but change will only be skin-deep, not soul-transforming.

Do *not* try to make other people 'get it'

A variant on this problem of learning new values is a lesson about effective implementation, taken from the history of cell-church development. It bred two rival theories of how the principles should be applied. This debate, which is still live, has important implications for any church or diocese wanting to introduce seven sacred spaces thinking.

One theory, known as 'big bang', held that the way forward was for the values to be taught to the receiving congregation until the leader was convinced they were understood.[3] Then all prior house groups, at a predetermined stroke, were changed to become 'cell groups'. This strategy rightly put an early emphasis on values. The centralised implementation was to prevent infinite delay, of which church people are capable. What was noticeable was that its exponents taught it took several years of subsequent practice for the newly renamed groups to truly live out the new life. As time has gone on, I notice that estimates of the years needed to make that change have increased from five to seven and from seven to ten.

The alternative theory was called 'prototype'. Once more the values were explained to the wider congregation, but only as a taster to see who was energised by this and wanted to take it forward. Chosen volunteers then formed an initial group with the founder and set out on the cell-church journey. The rest of the congregation remained in the prior patterns of church life. As the prototype group grew in practice and confidence, so their quality of life was noticed outside the group. The initial members then became group leaders for further voluntary groups. The start was smaller and it took years for the influence to spread, with some congregation members never adopting the new way.[4]

I think that the first style is benevolent dictatorship, whereas the second is consensual leadership. The first tends to the organisational and the second to the organic. The first relies on the limited impact arising from offering formal learning; the second route chooses learning by the messier but more interpersonal way of apprenticeship. In the end, the first is well-intended imposition, while the second models the vulnerability of being vocational. With such a list of contrasts, I link the second approach to the monastic roots of the seven sacred spaces.

The pattern of joining by vocation and calling fits with monasticism. It was deliberately never easy to join. 'Do not grant newcomers to the monastic life an easy entry,' says Benedict (58.1). He specifies that to begin with they knock on the monastery door for four to five days! Today, Northumbria Community have a novitiate that typically takes two years. This is about discerning a calling, not trying out some new church trick from the vicar.

I fear that imposing the seven spaces on a group, congregation or diocese is like changing the labels on a bottle, but not its contents. Centralised imposition will lead to much energy from the centre being expended, but transformation at the edges will be minimal.

Take care where you sow

In that denominations, congregations and clergy can be resistant to change, the seven spaces have no privileged position to escape this problem. With other change processes I've seen over a longer period, sowing seeds in specific places has had more effectiveness.

One way is to identify those local congregations that know there is a need of change and exhibit some willingness and resource to do so. This has been a strategy emerging in the 2010s around some dioceses in the Anglican Communion.[5] A second possible approach would be offering this thinking to ordinands or first-time incumbents. By such means seeds of change to existing practice could be sown for the future. A third way is to explore it with pioneers.

Whichever way, find those who want to live life more fully in Christ and a seed bed is unearthed. Among these three groups, a healthy sense of dissatisfaction may exist. Rowan Williams identifies this in the earliest manifestation of monasticism, with the desert fathers and mothers:

> The early monks and nuns moved off into communities of the desert because they weren't convinced that the church in its 'ordinary' manifestations showed with any clarity what the Church was supposed to be about… what humanity really was when it was in touch with God through Jesus Christ.[6]

What the seven spaces do offer us

Connections across big questions

The quotation from Williams not only links the seven sacred spaces to a healthy questioning of how satisfactory current church life is, but it also reveals a characteristic connection between some of its foundational disciplines and wider issues beyond church.

Broad questions like 'What is it to be human?' and 'How can people take a holistic approach to life?' are touched by the seven spaces and what they enable. Equally the spaces help us to explore related questions: 'How is life in Christ found and sustained?' and 'How might we reimagine church?' Thus they tread a path across big-sounding disciplines like anthropology, ecology, soteriology, Trinity and ecclesiology. This is not surprising, for Christians have always held that the fullness of life in God through Christ and being fully human considerably overlap. The commonality is humans being understood as being in the image of God. God's intention, whether seen through the language of mission or that of the kingdom, is the restoration of that image, as well as of the whole creation.

It is then both vital and appropriate that the seven spaces do not remain locked up within, or only applied to, church circles. They provide, though doubtless needing some translation in partnership with those outside of church, a way of exploring what makes human beings flourish, how communities are built and how sympathetic architecture can helpfully assist the diversity of ways in which people need to connect – to eat, study, work, decide, meet, play, pray – and also need to be alone. This variety can expect that particular spaces may be championed differently by educators, librarians, cooks, gardeners, ecologists, those in government, liturgists, sociologists, spiritual directors and so on. Part of the point is that we need them all, and an emphasis on any one, to the exclusion of the others, is a mistake.

Balance across the seven and interconnections between them will be where some of the energy lies. The role of food in relation to deciding, meeting, playing, studying and working is an obvious example, and its presence can markedly change the dynamics. Food is an inherent part of the Alpha Course in a church case, as are state banquets in intergovernmental encounters.

Five images of the seven sacred spaces

1 A diet

The seven sacred spaces approach is like a diet, in several ways. Only reading the diet sheet will do nothing. Adopting its recommendations for a short time will fail to change life patterns, though it may shed some excess weight for that limited time. Apparently, millions of pounds are spent by people going on diets and yet, no sooner has the period of the diet ended than many people go back to old habits. Whatever health had been gained is quickly lost, and whatever excess weight had been lost is rapidly regained.

All good diets exhibit balance. Here, adopting only parts of the seven sacred spaces will be in danger of imbalance. The analogy of a diet connects to the proper search for sustainable health. Only the diet, the whole diet and nothing but the diet offers a new way of living. This diet is about life in Christ, and being human, that has been tested over time. This assumes the grace-filled pursuit of the virtues linked to the places, for the places in themselves are not magic.

Having a diet is not the point of life. But it may help life to find its point, through being a healthier person. Archbishop Barry Morgan of Wales in his 2011 mission statement for Llandaff diocese, who were using the seven spaces, spoke of developing ministry and discipleship of all God's people, so that 'transformed ourselves, we might play our part in helping transform God's world'. That is the spirit in which the seven spaces should be approached. They are but a means of grace to a far greater end. Yet the means can be significant.

2 A shared language

The seven sacred spaces approach offers a shared vocabulary or common language. It creates a working shorthand. All disciplines engender a common specialist vocabulary. Theology uses terms such as 'perichoresis' or 'eschatology'. Car manufacturers refer to functions like ABS or traction control. This advantage of shared terms has to be held in tension with the need to translate that specialist language to others. To use the shared language well, the teachers of this way of thinking will need to be able to move fluently across traditional monastic language about the spaces and also dynamic translations suited to a context. They will also encourage practitioners to do the same.

Shared language can also be a way in which diverse teams and groups spot commonalities and conversations begin. I have noticed that when the seven spaces and their roles are outlined, it begins conversations rather than closing them. It is as though the spaces each evoke pictures that open possibilities. People recognise the spaces in their wider experience of life and want to contribute to the understanding of their function. Groups given the task to discuss their meaning or application find energy and contribute readily.

3 A lens

The image of the lens suggests other significant gains: bringing reality into focus, delivering people from being short-sighted, being able to 'see what's going on', and interpreting life in a different yet better way. Some churches and their leaders struggle to find ways forward. They seem to lack confidence in growing in community life and outgoing mission. They know the kingdom beckons them onward but are uncertain how to do that. To see a way forward would be good. Put these specs on and many other things become clear. To have a sharper view of what it is to be human, how a more whole way of living may be followed, how life in Christ may be gained and lived out, how quality community is grown and what church is made of – these are significant gains in vision.

However, heed the warning that to be unaware of the lens is to imagine that what you see is exactly like that. A lens is neither infallible nor objective. There may be things it does not spot, and the lens-wearer also plays a part in deciding what to do with the new information. Hence, use of the seven spaces needs always to be held humbly with the acknowledged need of discernment. Discerning is a word related to perceiving or seeing.

4 A ring road

As I have written the book, I have been aware that several chapters open up enormous subjects: Chapel and what is worship; Cell and how does one pray; Garden and the world of work; Refectory and exercising hospitality. Each of those big topics is like a major road leading off from its named space. Equally a developed understanding of each wider topic feeds into a profounder view of the particular named space. So I imagine the seven spaces as more than just a roundabout, where all that happens is that these major roads intersect. It is more like a ring road that has its own life, serving a city. It acts as a community hub from which many directions can be explored and returned to. To connect all these big wider topics is valuable.

5 A portal

Portals are a widely used image for mysterious but significant entrances. They exist in 'The Chronicles of Narnia', the 'Harry Potter' series, *Doctor Who* and *Star Trek*. You can't always see the door. Indeed, it may not always be unlocked. Like Hogwarts' Room of Requirement, a portal may move around and yet appear when needed. In the Narnia stories, they are always means of connecting and mark the beginning of a greater journey on the other side. Portals are ports; they are places of connection, beginnings and departures. They are entrances to their own worlds – take King's Cross platform 9¾, for example. They are rarely gateways to sheer paradise or heaven; more often they open to the challenge of pursuing the good amid the baleful presence of the bad. Yet by themselves, when viewed from outside, they are unimpressive. You cannot see the adventure, journey and discovery hidden beyond the portal. The seven sacred spaces are but portals – to deeper shared life in Christ.

Three applications

We now have a new chance to learn again and to refashion all Christian communities.

1 Any prospective reordering of a church building should include these standard questions. Which of the seven spaces are well served? Which are there but unrecognised? Which are missing altogether? We should ensure that, at the least, the function of all six corporate ones are provided for the greater health of that church family.

2 The seven sacred spaces could serve as a clergy appraisal tool and become one standard way to assess the health of churches and their leaders. Leaders could consider the balance in their individual lives across the spaces and to assess, with local lay leaders, the presence, absence and balance of the seven in the life of the congregation. It should include how the spaces are doing in the surrounding parish or community. This approach would have most value if it was repeated every few years, seeing progress and continuing to make necessary adjustments.

3 We are seeing fresh expressions of church come to birth. For them it will matter to know these dynamics, for being church is far more than occupying a type of building; it is living the life of the Christian community that inhabits and is fed by various locations. Why grow something which is lopsided, lacking one of these seven functions? I think it is legitimate for a young church to say of themselves, 'We cannot express all these dimensions immediately.' But over time, unless the search for the seven is an aspiration crystallising out, some aspects will be missing and some elements too dominant. Either way it will matter.

Seven sacred spaces is how things are

This book has tried to offer a wide range of evidence. There is my own story of their gradual showing themselves to me. From there I unpacked what each one does. Seven chapters then delved into the support for each one found in the monastic Rules, why they are important and what is needed to live them well. Attention to their purpose is key rather than erecting a place for each.

I also put a case that it is still valid to learn from monasticism and how it is always called to renew the whole church. I connected all this to ways they continue to appear in everyday life, how they express a way of being more fully human in community and how they open our eyes to see a richer way of understanding what church is. These are important gains. I also argued that the spaces, despite what critics say, do include mission and that they intersect with emerging ways to reconsider discipleship.

Coming from centuries of practice, this was never mere theory. Today there is wide practical take-up of the spaces, shown by a range of stories. They worked for an individual, in a diocese, in a ministry centre, in a young church, in art, in reordering a church building, in new monasticism and in Messy Church.

The seven sacred spaces come from a trustworthy source. They have a significant role to play, and a wide range of settings have shown they work and bring life. This is not the last word on the subject, but it is a promising first one. I suggest it is time for all expressions of church to learn from this wisdom of the ages. Not for nothing have I dubbed them as sacred.

Notes

Chapter 1

1 George Lings, *Reproducing Churches* (BRF, 2017).
2 P.G. Wodehouse, *Cocktail Time* (Penguin, 1987), p. 9.
3 From John Bunyan's *The Pilgrim's Progress*.
4 It is technically known as a 'font for immersion' by Anglicans, as a baptistery is the whole room that contains it.
5 These are still available as PDF files from Church Army. The full Carpenters Arms story is number 7.

Chapter 2

1 This chronology is taken from a translation of *The Philokalia* (Faber and Faber, 1983), p. 72.
2 For many examples, see Rowan Williams, *Silence and Honey Cakes: The wisdom of the desert* (Lion, 2003), ch. 1.
3 All quotations from the Rule of Benedict are taken from Timothy Fry (ed.), *The Rule of St Benedict in English* (The Liturgical Press, 1981).
4 Mary Margaret Funk OSB has written five successive books on this, beginning with *Thoughts Matter: Discovering the spiritual journey* (Liturgical Press, 2013), in which she unpacks both the vices and their treatment.
5 For a brilliant unpacking of this spiritual insight see Mark Clavier, *On Consumer Culture, Identity, the Church and the Rhetorics of Delight* (T&T Clark, 2019).
6 Joan Chittister OSB, *The Rule of Benedict: Insights for the ages* (Crossroad, 1992), p. 15. Allusively by Alasdair Macintyre in *After Virtue: A study in moral theology* (Notre Dame Press, 1981), ending on p. 263 with: 'We are waiting not for Godot, but for another – doubtless very different – St Benedict.' Also Laurence Freeman OSB in the Introduction to Williams, *Silence and Honeycakes*, pp. 10–11.
7 Esther De Waal, *Living with Contradiction: An introduction to Benedictine spirituality* (Canterbury Press, 1997), p. 21.

8 Chittister, *The Rule of Benedict*, pp. 22–23.

9 See Thomas O'Loughlin, *Celtic Theology: Humanity, world, and God in early Irish writings* (Continuum, 2005).

10 Uinseann Ó Maidín OCR, *The Celtic Monk: Rules and writings of early Irish monks* (Cistercian Publications, 1996), p. 8.

11 **catholicireland.net/columbanus-in-his-own-words**. Accessed 7 March 2019.

12 Thomas Cahill, *How the Irish Saved Civilisation: The untold story of Ireland's heroic role from the fall of Rome to the rise of Medieval Europe* (Anchor Books, 1995), p. 184. Page 156 furnishes a sketch.

13 It is recorded in Ó Maidín, *The Celtic Monk*.

14 Colmcille 16; Carthage, duties of the Celi De, 6 and 10; Celi De (Ó Maidín, *The Celtic Monk*, p. 92); Tallaght, 54a and 65.

15 Brother Ramon SSF, *Franciscan Spirituality* (SPCK, 1997), p. 66 uses this word 'adventure'.

16 David Flood and Thadee Matura, *The Birth of a Movement: A study of the first Rule of St. Francis* (Franciscan Herald Press, 1975), p. xviii.

17 Bishop John Moorman, *A History of the Franciscan Order: From its origins to the year 1517* (Clarendon Press, 1968), p. 14.

18 Ramon, *Franciscan Spirituality*, p. 61.

19 Moorman, *A History of the Franciscan Order*, pp. 16–17.

20 Flood and Matura, *The Birth of a Movement*, p. xix.

21 Ramon, *Franciscan Spirituality*, pp. 36, 6.

22 *The Testament of Francis* v. 24: 'Let the brothers be careful not to receive in any way churches or poor dwellings, or anything else built for them…'

23 Ramon, *Franciscan Spirituality*, p. 117.

24 Ramon, *Franciscan Spirituality*, p. 81.

25 Ramon, *Franciscan Spirituality*, p. 25.

26 Ramon, *Franciscan Spirituality*, p. 61.

27 *The Daily Office SSF* (Society of St Francis, 1992), pp. 301–11.

28 Flood and Matura, *The Birth of a Movement*, pp. 116–17.

29 Members of this Indian community returned to England and played a founding role in the modern Anglican Franciscan story in the early 20th century.

30 *The Daily Office SSF*, p. 302, day 6.

31 Ian Morgan Cron, *Chasing Francis: A pilgrim's tale* (Nav Press, 2006).

Chapter 3

1   Christopher Jamison, *Finding Sanctuary: Monastic steps for everyday life* (Weidenfeld and Nicholson, 2006), p. 41.

2   I am grateful to a friend, Jane Truman, for making me aware of this varied set of routes, which is teased out far more in Gary L. Thomas, *Sacred Pathways: Discover your soul's path to God* (Thomas Nelson, 1996).

3   Joan Chittister OSB, *The Rule of Benedict: Insights for the ages* (Crossroad, 1992), p. 61.

4   Jamison, *Finding Sanctuary*, p. 40.

5   Jamison, *Finding Sanctuary*, p. 41.

6   Chittister, *The Rule of Benedict*, p. 75.

7   Meg Funk explains compunction as the tension between the desire for God yet angst of being at distance from him. See Mary Margaret Funk OSB, *Thoughts Matter: Discovering the spiritual journey* (Liturgical Press, 2013), p. 185.

8   Uinseann Ó Maidín OCR, *The Celtic Monk: Rules and writings of early Irish monks* (Cistercian Publications, 1996), Ailbe 8a, 20, 26 and 49, respectively.

9   Ó Maidín, *The Celtic Monk*, p. 32, Comgall 6 and 11.

10   Ó Maidín, *The Celtic Monk*, p. 69, Carthage, duties of the Celi De 4, and p. 72, Carthage, order of meals 27.

11   Oliver Davies (ed.), *Celtic Spirituality* (Paulist Press, 1999), Columbanus sections 7, 8.

12   Ó Maidín, *The Celtic Monk*, p. 69, Carthage, duties of the Celi De 6.

13   Brother Ramon SSF, *Franciscan Spirituality* (SPCK, 1997), p. 88.

14   Funk, *Thoughts Matter* , p. 124.

15   Henri J.M. Nouwen, *The Way of the Heart: Desert spirituality and contemporary ministry* (2nd edition, DLT, 1990), extracts from pp. 22–23, 27–28.

16   Nouwen, *The Way of the Heart*, p. 25.

17   Rowan Williams, *Silence and Honey Cakes: The wisdom of the desert* (Lion, 2003), pp. 52–53.

18   Henri J.M. Nouwen, *Making All Things New*, quoted in Richard Foster, *Devotional Classics: Selected readings for individuals and groups* (Harper, 2000), p. 136.

19   Andrew Roberts, *Holy Habits* (Malcolm Down, 2016).

20   Williams, *Silence and Honey Cakes*, p. 68.

21 Funk, *Thoughts Matter*, p. 123, and *Tools Matter: Beginning the spiritual journey* (Liturgical Press, 2013), p. 107.

22 Compare the master's praise of the servant with ten talents (Luke 19:17), the centurion's praise of his own servant (Matthew 8:9), Mary's instructions to servants at the wedding in Cana (John 2:5), and the protestation of dutiful obedient servants (Luke 17:10).

23 Henri J.M. Nouwen, *Making All Things New: An invitation to the spiritual life* (HarperCollins, 1981), p. 136; Jamison, *Finding Sanctuary*, p. 76, and Ramon, *Franciscan Spirituality*, p. 73, both concur.

24 Brother Lawrence, *The Practice of the Presence of God*, translated by E.M. Blaiklock (Hodder and Stoughton, 1985), p. 24.

25 Funk, *Thoughts Matter*, p. 2. Another overview of the centrality of Cell is found in Northumbria Community, *Celtic Daily Prayer*, Book Two (Collins, 2015), pp. 1528–48.

26 Funk, *Thoughts Matter*, p. 124.

27 Mark Clavier, *On Consumer Culture, Identity, the Church and the Rhetorics of Delight* (T&T Clark, 2019).

28 Tom Smail is rightly critical of Augustine at this point, in that limiting the Spirit to being the love between Father and Son reduces the personhood of the Spirit. *Like Father Like Son: The Trinity imaged in our humanity* (Paternoster, 2005), pp. 75, 81.

29 Lawrence, *The Practice of the Presence of God*, pp. 19–30.

30 J. P. Camus, *The Spirit of Francois de Sales*, translated by C.F. Kelley (Longmans, Green and Co, 1953), p. 5.

31 Funk, *Tools Matter*, p. 108.

32 Dietrich Bonhoeffer, *Letters and Papers from Prison* (Collins, Fontana, 1970), p. 173.

Chapter 4

1 Brother Ramon SSF, *Franciscan Spirituality* (SPCK, 1997), p. 117.

2 Ramon, *Franciscan Spirituality*, p. 118.

3 Dietrich Bonhoeffer, *Life Together* (SCM, 1954), pp. 59–61.

4 Christopher Jamison, *Finding Sanctuary: Monastic steps for everyday life* (Weidenfeld and Nicholson, 2006), pp. 54–55.

5 See Steve Aisthorpe, *The Invisible Church: Learning from the experiences of churchless Christians* (St Andrew Press, 2016) for patterns in Scotland. I noted something similar regarding the Northumbria Community members in chapter 10.

6 Uinseann Ó Maidín OCR, *The Celtic Monk: Rules and writings of early Irish monks* (Cistercian Publications, 1996), Ailbe 10, 16 and 22.

7 Ó Maidín, *The Celtic Monk*, Carthage, the duties of the Celi De 1, p. 69.

8 The Rule of Augustine 2.11 concurs.

9 In older, superseded counting systems it is called Psalm 118.

10 Ó Maidín, *The Celtic Monk*: Ailbe 17, 19.

11 Oliver Davies (ed.), *Celtic Spirituality* (Paulist Press, 1999), pp. 52–53, and p. 343, for the citation.

12 Joan Chittister OSB, *The Rule of Benedict: Insights for the ages* (Crossroad, 1992), p. 90.

13 Ó Maidín, *The Celtic Monk*, Comgall 4, p. 32.

14 The Rule of Benedict 16.1, taken from a literal application of Psalm 119:164.

15 Chittister, *The Rule of Benedict*, pp. 85, 76.

16 Northumbria Community, *Celtic Daily Prayer*, Book Two (Collins, 2015), p. 875.

17 Lynne Truss, *Eats, Shoots and Leaves* (4th Estate, 2009).

18 Chittister, *The Rule of Benedict*, p. 88.

19 *The Daily Office SSF* (SSF, 1992), p. vii. Otherwise known as *Celebrating Common Prayer*.

20 Mark Earey, *Beyond Common Worship: Anglican identity and liturgical diversity* (SCM, 2013). Read the brilliant concise conclusion in pp. 139–41.

21 Liturgical Commission of the Church of England, *Patterns for Worship*, report GS 898 (Church House Publishing, 1989), pp. 1–8.

22 Earey, *Beyond Common Worship*, pp. 86–91 and Steven Croft (ed.), *The Future of the Parish System: Shaping the Church of England for the twenty-first century* (Church House Publishing, 2006), p. 180.

23 Chittister, *The Rule of Benedict*, p. 140.

24 Ramon, *Franciscan Spirituality*, p. 90.

Chapter 5

1 This is where the eleventh-century Cistercian reform of Benedictine life took place.

2 The Rule of Benedict 66.8: 'We wish this rule to be read often in the community.'

3 Christopher Jamison, *Finding Sanctuary: Monastic steps for everyday life* (Weidenfeld and Nicholson, 2006), p. 99.

4 Rowan Williams, *Silence and Honey Cakes: The wisdom of the desert* (Lion, 2003), p. 29.

5 Williams, *Silence and Honey Cakes*, pp. 22–23.

6 Williams, *Silence and Honey Cakes*, p. 28.

7 Williams, *Silence and Honey Cakes*, p. 24.

8 Private email correspondence, April 2015.

9 Uinseann Ó Maidín OCR, *The Celtic Monk: Rules and writings of early Irish monks* (Cistercian Publications, 1996), Ailbe 25a, 33.

10 Ó Maidín, *The Celtic Monk*, Ailbe 41a.

11 Ó Maidín, *The Celtic Monk*, Ailbe 41a, 41b.

12 Ó Maidín, *The Celtic Monk*, Ailbe 27d.

13 Ó Maidín, *The Celtic Monk*, Carthage 1–20.

14 Brother Ramon SSF, *Franciscan Spirituality* (SPCK, 1997), p. 87.

15 Currently there are about half a dozen provinces, depending on geography and the density of distribution of brothers: Europe is one, the Americas another, while Papua New Guinea has its own.

16 Colin Patterson, *How to Learn through Conflict* (Grove Pastoral 96, 2003). Later he wrote *Embracing Conflict* (Grove Leadership 30, 2017) on learning through Jesus as a model.

Chapter 6

1 Dietrich Bonhoeffer, *Life Together* (SCM, 2008), p. 58.

2 In the understanding of the Rule of Benedict, monks called to be solitaries are those who have already mastered the demands of being in monasteries (1.3–4).

3 Tom Smail, *LLike Father Like Son: The Trinity imaged in our humanity* (Paternoster, 2005).

4 Rowan Williams, *Silence and Honey Cakes: The wisdom of the desert* (Lion, 2003), p. 51.

5 Williams, *Silence and Honey Cakes*, p. 58.

6 John Michael Talbot, *The Lessons of St Francis: How to bring simplicity and spirituality into your daily life* (Plume, 1998), pp. 75ff.

7 Williams, *Silence and Honey Cakes*, p. 24.

8 Williams, *Silence and Honey Cakes*, p. 29.

9 Joan Chittister OSB, *The Rule of Benedict: Insights for the ages* (Crossroad, 1992), p. 71.

10 Christopher Jamison, *Finding Sanctuary: Monastic steps for everyday life* (Weidenfeld and Nicholson, 2006), p. 117.

11 Uinseann Ó Maidín OCR, *The Celtic Monk: Rules and writings of early Irish monks* (Cistercian Publications, 1996), Ailbe 4, 6, 12, 13, 15.

12 Ó Maidín, *The Celtic Monk*, Comgall 7, p. 32.

13 Ó Maidín, *The Celtic Monk*, Carthage 2, 3, 8, pp. 67–68.

14 Oliver Davies (ed.), *Celtic Spirituality* (Paulist Press, 1999), Columbanus, 1, 2, 5, 8, 9.

15 Brother Ramon SSF, *Franciscan Spirituality* (SPCK, 1997), p. 117.

16 Northumbria Community, *Celtic Daily Prayer*, Book 2 (Collins, 2015), pp. 1148–66, days 2, 4–8, 10, 31.

Chapter 7

1 At Hilfield Friary I discovered a moving poem by David Scott written for one of their families' camps, entitled: 'A long way from bread.' It is now published by the alarmingly named Bloodaxe Books – search for David Scott at **bloodaxebooks.com**.

2 The Quiet Garden Movement, begun by Revd Philip Roderick, draws upon this and is a welcome additional route for people to explore spirituality and for existing Christians to find ways to better balance a life beyond activism.

3 Sister Joyce CSF (ed.), *Walking in the Footsteps of Christ*, the historical documents of the Society of Saint Francis (SSF, 2003), pp. 42–48.

4 Uinseann Ó Maidín OCR, *The Celtic Monk: Rules and writings of early Irish monks* (Cistercian Publications, 1996), Colmcille 16 and Celi De, p. 92. This is echoed in Carthage 6, p. 69, and Columbanus, ch. 3: 'Every day we must pray, labour and read.'

5 Trevor Miller, Northumbria Community mother house manual, private paper, 2006, p. 3.

6 See Mary Margaret Funk OSB, *Thoughts Matter: Discovering the spiritual journey* (Liturgical Press, 2013), pp. 121–23, 128–29, and *Tools Matter: Beginning the spiritual journey* (Liturgical Press, 2013), pp. 49, 65.

7 Joan Chittister OSB, *The Rule of Benedict: Insights for the ages* (Crossroad, 1992), p. 132.

8 Brother Ramon SSF, *Franciscan Spirituality* (SPCK, 1997), p. 91.

9 Ramon, *Franciscan Spirituality*, pp. 126–48.

10 Ó Maidín, *The Celtic Monk*, Ailbe 9, 26.

11 Ó Maidín, *The Celtic Monk*, Ailbe 50.

12 Ó Maidín, *The Celtic Monk*, Colmcille 17.

13 licc.org.uk
14 Ó Maidín, *The Celtic Monk*, Colmcille 28
15 Ó Maidín, *The Celtic Monk*, Carthage, duties of the Celi De 10
16 Ó Maidín, *The Celtic Monk*, Celi De, p. 92.
17 Oliver Davies (ed.), *Celtic Spirituality* (Paulist Press, 1999), Columbanus, ch. 3, p. 248.
18 Brother Lawrence, *The Practice of the Presence of God*, translated by E.M. Blaiklock (Hodder and Stoughton, 1985), p. 23

Chapter 8

1 Trevor Miller, Northumbria Community mother house manual, private paper, 2006, p. 1.
2 Quoted in Mary Margaret Funk OSB, *Thoughts Matter: Discovering the spiritual journey* (Liturgical Press, 2013), p. 130.
3 This is covered by George Lings, *Discernment in Mission: Navigation aids for mission-shaped processes*, Encounters on the Edge 30 (Church Army, 2006), **churcharmy.org/Articles/516326/What_we_do/Research_Unit/Publications.aspx#Encounters**.
4 Joan Chittister OSB, *The Rule of Benedict: Insights for the ages* (Crossroad, 1992), p. 95.
5 Francis was against having cellarers, not for their function but because it reintroduced rank.
6 Chittister, *The Rule of Benedict*, p. 110
7 Chittister, *The Rule of Benedict*, p. 148.
8 Chittister, *The Rule of Benedict*, p. 143.
9 Chittister, *The Rule of Benedict*, p. 118.
10 Named as such in Rule of Ailbe 28, Carthage refectory section and Tallaght 80.
11 Uinseann Ó Maidín OCR, *The Celtic Monk: Rules and writings of early Irish monks* (Cistercian Publications, 1996), Ailbe 34.
12 Ó Maidín, *The Celtic Monk*, Ailbe 42.
13 Ó Maidín, *The Celtic Monk*, Ailbe 41
14 Ó Maidín, *The Celtic Monk*, Ailbe 21. Columbanus concurs, ch. 3.
15 Ó Maidín, *The Celtic Monk*, Carthage, refectory section, 2, p. 70.
16 Christopher Jamison, *Finding Sanctuary: Monastic steps for everyday life* (Weidenfeld and Nicholson, 2006), p. 116.
17 Jamison, *Finding Sanctuary*, p. 117.
18 George Lings, *The Day of Small Things* (Church Army, 2016), p. 82.
19 Miller, Northumbria Community mother house manual, p. 1.

Chapter 9

1 Thomas Cahill, *How the Irish Saved Civilisation: The untold story of Ireland's heroic role from the fall of Rome to the rise of Medieval Europe* (Anchor Books, 1995), p. 156 contains a sketch plan of the Irish Monastery, and p. 184, a description of Iona's buildings. The seven places are all operative, though cloister must be inferred.

2 Uinseann Ó Maidín OCR, *The Celtic Monk: Rules and writings of early Irish monks* (Cistercian Publications, 1996), Ailbe 7, 20.

3 Ó Maidín, *The Celtic Monk*, Colmcille 16, p. 41.

4 Ó Maidín, *The Celtic Monk*, Carthage, duties of the Celi De, 6, 8.

5 Ó Maidín, *The Celtic Monk*, Tallaght 54a, 91.

6 Oliver Davies (ed.), *Celtic Spirituality* (Paulist Press, 1999), section 7 on the choir office.

7 Brother Ramon SSF, *Franciscan Spirituality* (SPCK, 1997), p. 25.

8 Ramon, *Franciscan Spirituality*, p. 19.

9 Christopher Jamison, *Finding Sanctuary: Monastic steps for everyday life* (Weidenfeld and Nicholson, 2006), p. 60.

10 Joan Chittister OSB, *The Rule of Benedict: Insights for the ages* (Crossroad, 1992), p. 133.

11 Jamison, *Finding Sanctuary*, p. 62.

12 Jamison, *Finding Sanctuary*, pp. 63–66.

13 Rabbi Jonathan Sacks, *Not in God's Name: Confronting religious violence* (Hodder, 2015), pp. 16–17 develops both changes further.

Chapter 10

1 Mark Mills-Powell (ed.), *Setting the Church of England Free* (John Hunt, 2003), p. 47.

2 Owen Chadwick, *The Reformation* (Penguin Books, 1968), p. 45.

3 Dietrich Bonhoeffer, *The Cost of Discipleship* (SCM, 1971), p. 40.

4 Bonhoeffer, *The Cost of Discipleship*, pp. 38–39.

5 Chadwick, *The Reformation*, p. 13.

6 Chadwick, *The Reformation*, p. 33. The latter group because their methods 'seemed to be obsolete'.

7 Christopher Donaldson, *Martin of Tours: The shaping of Celtic spirituality* (Canterbury Press, 1997), p. 30.

8 This is also true in the USA and in Catholic Europe, but this book cannot cover the worldwide spread. One US account is Rutba House (ed.), *School(s) for Conversion: 12 marks of a new monasticism*

(Cascade, 2005). I have not used it because I am not convinced that a number of their twelve cited marks, though all noble, are universal and apply in England.

9 Ian Bradley, *Colonies of Heaven: Celtic models for today's church* (DLT, 2000), p. 49.

10 Ray Simpson, *A Pilgrim Way: New Celtic monasticism for everyday people* (Kevin Mayhew, 2005); **aidanandhilda.org.uk**

11 In 2019 there were thought to be around 460 Companions, around 90 exploring becoming one and 1,410 Friends.

12 One account of its history and values from founding until 2009 is George Lings, *Northumbria Community: Matching monastery and mission*, Encounters on the Edge 29 (Church Army, 2009), still available from the Community or at **churcharmy.org/Articles/517054/What_we_do/Research_Unit/Encounters_on_the.aspx**. In earlier years the leadership was twofold: an abbot (monastery) and a bishop-type figure (mission).

13 For a summary of Iona's story, ethos, scope and rule see Bradley, *Colonies of Heaven*, pp. 45–48.

14 'Charism' means that special combination of calling and character which makes it one of God's gifts to the church.

15 Rowan Williams, *Why Study the Past? The quest for the historical church* (DLT, 2005), p. 55.

16 Henri J.M. Nouwen, *Life of the Beloved: Spiritual living in a secular world* (Hodder and Stoughton, 2002), p. 69.

17 For effective spiritual countering of this force, see Mark Clavier, *On Consumer Culture, Identity, the Church and the Rhetorics of Delight* (T&T Clark, 2019).

18 Hugh Ellis, 'Fires of heaven', in Mills-Powell, *Setting the Church of England Free*, p. 128.

19 Rowan Williams, *Silence and Honey Cakes: The wisdom of the desert* (Lion, 2003), p. 23.

20 See Antonio Romano's inspiring book *The Charism of the Founders: The person and the charism of founders in contemporary theological reflection* (St Paul's Press, 1994), p. 35.

21 Romano, *The Charism of the Founders*, p. 53.

22 Brother Ramon SSF, *Franciscan Spirituality* (SPCK, 1997), p. 50.

23 Romano, *The Charism of the Founders*, p. 60.

24 Romano, *The Charism of the Founders*, p. 61.

25 Gerald Arbuckle, *Refounding the Church: Dissent for leadership* (Geoffrey Chapman, 1993), p. 155.

26 G.B. Kelly and B. Nelson, *A Testament to Freedom: The essential writings of Dietrich Bonhoeffer* (Harper, 1995), p. 424, and often quoted in Northumbria Community materials.

27 The Rule and its monasteries are credited with preserving western culture.

28 Alasdair MacIntyre, *After Virtue: A study in moral theology* (Notre Dame Press, 1984), p. 263.

29 Bradley, *Colonies of Heaven*, p. xi.

30 Ramon, *Franciscan Spirituality*, p. 95.

31 That story is summarised in Ramon, *Franciscan Spirituality*, pp. 90–91.

32 Brother Samuel SSF, an article on mission and community in *Transmission* (British and Foreign Bible Society, 1998).

33 The classic exposition of this complementary difference is Ralph D. Winter, 'The two structures of God's redemptive mission', *Missiology: An international review* 2:1, pp. 121–39. It is one essay in Ralph Winter and Stephen Hawthorne (eds), *Perspectives on the World Christian Movement: A reader* (William Carey, 2009), p. 244ff. It is also available at **undertheiceberg.com/wp-content/uploads/2006/04/Sodality-Winter%20on%20Two%20Structures1.pdf**.

34 For a contemporary explanation of the classic four marks, see Graham Cray, *Mission-Shaped Church* (Church House Publishing, 2004), pp. 96–99. A longer one is found in Mike Moynagh, *Church for Every Context* (SCM, 2012), pp. 104–18.

35 Jean Vanier, *Community and Growth* (DLT, 1979), p. 87.

36 Bradley, *Colonies of Heaven*, p. 55.

37 Ramon, *Franciscan Spirituality*, pp. 72–73.

38 Dietrich Bonhoeffer, *Life Together* (SCM, 2008), p. 58.

Chapter 11

1 Joan Chittister OSB, *The Rule of Benedict: Insights for the ages* (Crossroad, 1992), p. 19.

2 Christian Schwarz, *Natural Church Development* (BCGA, 1996), pp. 22–37.

3 Jean Vanier, *Community and Growth* (DLT, 1979), p. 12.

4 Justin Welby, *Reimagining Britain: Foundations for hope* (Bloomsbury Continuum, 2018), p. 3.

Chapter 12

1 Graham Cray, *Mission-Shaped Church* (Church House Publishing, 2004), p. 99.
2 Oliver Davies (ed.), *Celtic Spirituality* (Paulist Press, 1999), p. 38.
3 Brother Ramon SSF, *Franciscan Spirituality* (SPCK, 1997), pp. 8, 57.
4 Duane Arnold and C. George Fry, *Francis: A call to conversion* (Cantilever, 1988), p. 50, cited in Ramon, *Franciscan Spirituality*, p. 62.
5 Gerald Arbuckle, *Refounding the Church: Dissent for leadership* (Geoffrey Chapman, 1993), pp. 158–63.

Chapter 13

1 David Watson, *Discipleship* (Hodder and Stoughton, 1983), pp. 13, 16.
2 For example, Dietrich Bonhoeffer, *The Cost of Discipleship* (SCM, 1948) or Steven Croft, *Jesus' People: What the church should do next* (Church House Publishing, 2009).
3 Stephen Cherry, *Barefoot Disciple: Walking the way of passionate humility* (Continuum, 2011); Rowan Williams, *Being Disciples: Essentials of the Christian life* (SPCK, 2016).
4 This likeness is explored in Alan Kreider, *The Patient Ferment of the Early Church: The improbable rise of Christianity in the Roman Empire* (Baker Academic, 2016).
5 Lucy Peppiatt, *The Disciple: On becoming truly human* (Cascade, 2012); Cherry, *Barefoot Disciple*, p. 12.
6 I am indebted for this view to Ted Ward, Lois McKinney-Douglas, and John M. Dettoni, 'Effective learning in non-formal modes', *Common Ground Journal* 11:1 (Autumn 2013), pp. 32–37. Ward was professor of education at Michigan State University.
7 Cherry, *Barefoot Disciple*, p. 10; his italics.
8 Peppiatt, *The Disciple*, p. 138.

Chapter 14

1 Kenneth J. Gergen, quoted in James Holstein and Jaber Gubrium, *The Self We Live By: Narrative identity in a postmodern world* (OUP, 2000), pp. 58–60.
2 Holstein and Gubrium, *The Self We Live By*, p. 59. Italics added.

Chapter 15

1 Mary Margaret Funk OSB, *Humility Matters: Toward purity of heart* (Liturgical Press, 2013), p. xxii.
2 Comment on this tendency is noted in Paul Bayes, *Mission-Shaped Church*, Grove Evangelism Series 67 (Grove, 2004), pp. 24–27, and George Lings, *Messy Church: Ideal for all ages?*, Encounters on the Edge 46 (Church Army, 2008), p. 6.
3 Advocates included American authors, such as Bill Beckham and Ralph Neighbour, but also English ones in Phil Potter and Howard Astin.
4 A parish following this pattern led by Paul Bayes was reported in Hampshire; George Lings, *Soft Cell*, Encounters on the Edge 20 (Church Army, 2002).
5 Toronto, Sydney, London, Chester and possibly other dioceses have taken steps down this kind of road.
6 Rowan Williams, *Silence and Honey Cakes: The wisdom of the desert* (Lion, 2003), p. 23.

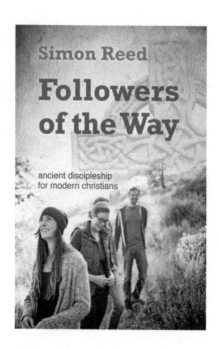

What discipleship means and how we help people to become true disciples is one of the most pressing issues in today's church. In simple terms discipleship is about connecting more deeply with God and connecting God with the whole of life, a life-long process for which we require long-term skills rather than just short-term courses. The Celtic and Desert Christians, drawing on Old and New Testament practices, taught and modelled how to do this through the practice of living by a Way of Life.

Followers of the Way
Ancient discipleship for modern Christians
Simon Reed
978 0 85746 538 2 £7.99

brfonline.org.uk

As Simon Reed explored the Celtic roots of the Christian faith, he came to realise that the third millennium church has much in common with the first millennium church, and more importantly, much to learn from it. In *Creating Community*, he introduces us to a new but at the same time very old way of being church which is based upon three core elements: a Way of Life, a network of Soul Friends, and a rhythm of prayer. The book shows how the rediscovery of these elements by Christians today offers a vital key that not only helps to bring believers to lasting maturity but also creates genuine community in an increasingly fragmented world.

Creating Community
Ancient ways for modern churches
Simon Reed
978 0 85746 009 7 £8.99

brfonline.org.uk

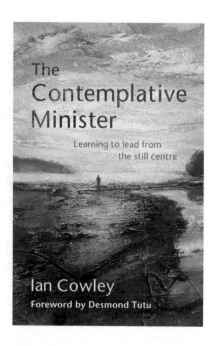

At one time Christian ministry offered the opportunity to spend your life
in the study of God's word, in reading and reflection, in prayer and sermon
preparation, and in the faithful pastoral care of a community. These
days there are very few jobs in full-time ministry which do not require a
heroic combination of stamina, multi-tasking and change management.
Drawing on his experience of developing and leading relevant training
programmes, Ian Cowley assesses the stresses and pressures of the job
and shows how to grow into a 'contemplative minister', prioritising a
relationship of deepening love with God.

The Contemplative Minister
Learning to lead from the still centre
Ian Cowley
978 0 85746 360 9 £8.99

brfonline.org.uk

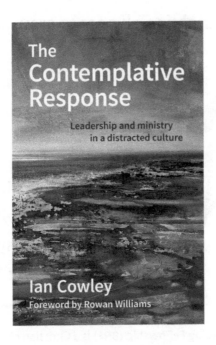

Following on from the success of *The Contemplative Minister*, Ian Cowley offers new insight and greater depth for church leaders in a distracted world. Cowley emphasises that the true self finds peace in resting in the love of God, and he encourages ministers to minister to themselves as well as to others, and to ensure that, in the peace that Jesus promises, their spiritual lives don't run dry amid the pressures of the job. A must-read for leaders wanting to stay the course.

The Contemplative Response
Leadership and ministry in a distracted culture
Ian Cowley
978 0 85746 656 3 £8.99

brfonline.org.uk

Enabling all ages to grow in faith

Anna Chaplaincy
Living Faith
Messy Church
Parenting for Faith

The Bible Reading Fellowship (BRF) is a Christian charity that resources individuals and churches. Our vision is to enable people of all ages to grow in faith and understanding of the Bible and to see more people equipped to exercise their gifts in leadership and ministry.

To find out more about our ministries and programmes, visit
brf.org.uk